BAD
EXAMPLES
from the
BIBLE

PATRICK HENRY REARDON

ANCIENT FAITH PUBLISHING
CHESTERTON, INDIANA

Bad Examples from the Bible
Copyright © 2025 Patrick Henry Reardon

Published by:
Ancient Faith Publishing
A Division of Ancient Faith Ministries
1050 Broadway, Suite 6
Chesterton, IN 46304

All translations from the original languages of Holy Scripture and other foreign language texts are my own. I cite the text in its underlying language in those places where it appears appropriate and instructive to do so. Old Testament quotations are made from both the Hebrew Bible transmitted in the Masoretic tradition and the canonical Greek text, the Septuagint (LXX), represented in the earliest Christian manuscripts. I rely on the standard published editions: Kittel and the Stuttgartensia for the Masoretic text (MT), Rahlfs for the Septuagint.

Book cover design by Bruce Petersen

ISBN: 978-1-955890-85-4

Library of Congress Control Number: 2025934700

Contents

Introduction   1

Part 1: The Soul Under Siege

Chapter 1: An Outline of Temptation   11

Chapter 2: Lurking Thought   15

Chapter 3: Impulsive Gratification   19

Chapter 4: The Love of the World   23

Chapter 5: Caution and the Sacred   27

Chapter 6: Coming Undone   32

Part 2: Frailty and Betrayal

Chapter 7: The Undisciplined Eye   39

Chapter 8: All in Perspective   43

Chapter 9: Enticement   48

Chapter 10: Youthful Folly   52

Chapter 11: The Shallow Heart   56

Chapter 12: A Stubborn Mind   61

Chapter 13: Cowardice   66

Chapter 14: The Habit of Guile   70

Part 3: Social Disorder

Chapter 15: Revising the Story   77

Chapter 16: Domestic Conspiracy   82

Chapter 17: Priestly Betrayal   86

Chapter 18: Nasty Religious People   90

Chapter 19: Industrial Waste   94

Chapter 20: Risking the Millstone   99

Part 4: Sin and Politics

Chapter 21: The Cultivation of Arrogance   107

Chapter 22: The Gospel and the Sword   111

Chapter 23: The Vengeful Soul   115

Chapter 24: The Pride of Life   119

Chapter 25: Hostile Power   124

Chapter 26: The Taste of Blood   128

Afterword   133

About the Author   137

Introduction

THE THEOLOGICAL UNITY of two distinct bodies of literature, the Old Testament and the Apostolic Writings—along with the propriety of binding them together in a single volume—is a fundamental tenet of the "faith once handed on to the saints" (Jude 1:3). Christian persuasion on this point rests on the conviction that Jesus fulfilled—brought to fullness—the promises contained in the Law and the Prophets. That is to say, the relationship between the Old and New Testaments is fundamentally Christological.

For this reason, the authority of the Old Testament is at the very heart of the mandate that Christ gave to the apostles; it is an integral part of the gospel itself and essential to the mission of the Church:

Then he said to them, "These are the words which I spoke to you while I was still with you, that all things must be fulfilled which were written in the Law of Moses and the Prophets and the Psalms concerning me." And he opened their understanding, that they might comprehend the Scriptures. Then he said to them, "Thus it is written, and thus it was necessary for the Christ to suffer and to rise from the dead the third day, and that repentance and remission of sins should be preached in his name to all nations, beginning at Jerusalem. And you are witnesses of these things." (Luke 24:44–48)

The Christian understanding of the Old Testament, therefore, is, at root, dogmatic; it is primarily concerned with the testimony of the Law and the Prophets to the person, work, and eternal significance of Jesus, the Son of God.

Tropology

In addition to the dogmatic sense of the Old Testament, the New Testament also recognizes in that ancient body of literature an important source of moral doctrine—a dimension that the Church Fathers called its ethical or tropological sense. This term refers to the Bible's existential, practical, and concrete application to the life of the believer. We read the Bible in order to know how we should live; it is a divine source of moral and ascetical teaching.

These practical moral applications in Holy Scripture do not always take the form of rules and exhortations. Often enough they appeal to concrete examples.

Saint James, for instance, seems to have been fond of this approach. He inquires, for instance, "Was not Abraham our father justified by works when he offered Isaac his son on the altar?" (2:21). Again, James asks, "Likewise, was not Rahab the harlot also justified by works when she received the messengers and sent them out by another way?" (2:25).

James switches from inquiry to exhortation when he cites yet another example from the Old Testament: "Indeed we count them blessed who endure. You have heard of the perseverance of Job and seen the Lord's purpose—that the Lord is very compassionate and merciful" (5:11). Once again, in his exhortation to fervent prayer, James summons another biblical example: "The effective, fervent prayer of a righteous man is capable of much. Elijah was a man like us (*homeopathes hemin*), and he prayed earnestly that it would not rain" (5:16b–17).

It is notable that the first of James's examples was Abraham, whom he called "the friend of God" (2:23). Abraham likewise served as a model of faith for the Apostle Paul (Rom. 4:1–22; Gal. 3:6–9) and the author of the Epistle to the Hebrews (6:11–14; 11:8–19).

In addition to Abraham, the author of Hebrews finds models of faith in Abel, Enoch, Noah, Sarah, Isaac, Jacob, Joseph, Moses, Rahab, Gideon, Barak, Samson, Jephthah, "also David and Samuel and the prophets" (11:4–32).

Types

I have been using the word *example* in our common and ideal sense of "model," someone to be emulated or imitated. Thus, Paul exhorted the Corinthians, "Be imitators (*mimetai*) of me, as I am of Christ" (1 Cor. 11:1).

The underlying Greek expression for our modern *example*, however, is more accurately *typos,* clearly the root of our English "type." Thus, in his treatment of the Israelites in the desert, Paul declared, "these things occurred as *typoi* of us" (1 Cor. 10:6). That is to say, the apostle discerned, in the account of Israel's journey through the desert, certain symbolic parallels with life in the Christian Faith. Thus, in the sacramental context of Baptism and the Eucharist, he told the Corinthians:

> I do not want you to be unaware that all our fathers were under the cloud, all passed through the sea, all were baptized in Moses in the cloud and in the sea, all ate the same spiritual food, and all drank the same spiritual drink. For they drank of that spiritual Rock that followed them, and that Rock was Christ. (1 Cor. 10:1–4)

Indeed, the whole story of Israel in the wilderness, Paul contended, was to be understood *typikos,* "by way of example" (1 Cor. 10:11).

Now, here is the ironic aspect of Paul's argument: The Israelites in the desert served as "typoi of us" in the sense that we should not imitate them; they are examples of what we must not become. Paul illustrates the point:

> And do not become idolaters as were some of them. As it is written, "The people sat down to eat and drink, and rose up to play." Nor let us commit sexual immorality, as some of them did, and in one day twenty-three thousand fell; nor let us test Christ, as some of them also tested, and were destroyed

by serpents; nor murmur, as some of them also murmured, and were destroyed by the destroyer. (1 Cor. 10:7–10)

Thus, in the one place where the Apostle Paul actually uses the word *examples,* he means bad examples.

Moralists have always known, of course, that we can learn as much from bad examples as from good ones. Esau and Doeg can instruct us as profitably as Isaac and Isaiah. There is as much to be learned from Joab as from Job. Sometimes only a brief mention of their stories suffices for the lesson, as when Jesus exhorted us, "Remember Lot's wife" (Luke 17:32).

Yes, for heaven's sake, let us never forget Lot's wife. There are so many bad examples we need to remember. Several of them are found in the present book.

But let us bear in mind, also, that not all bad examples come from bad people. Good people, too, can instruct us by their moral failings. For instance, Jesus was obliged to tell those two "sons of thunder," James and John—both of them deemed worthy to witness the Transfiguration and the Agony in the Garden—"You do not know of what manner of spirit you are" (Luke 9:55).

Examples are endless. On occasion Jacob could be as wily and deceptive as Odysseus, and Samson as irresponsible as Jack Aubrey. Barak, too, though listed among the heroes of Faith in Hebrews 11, hardly covered himself with glory when first the battle threatened. Baruch, Jeremiah's sorely tried secretary, was known to complain on occasion, and Jonah had his bad days, not all of them in the belly of the whale. As for the Apostle Paul, he found fault with at least three other saints: Peter, Barnabas, and Mark. Not all the saints are always at the top of their game.

In the present book, nonetheless—with few exceptions—I have concentrated on bad examples provided by bad people, sometimes very bad.

This book could easily be two or three times as long, but, frankly, such a lengthy concentration on evil would likely prove tedious at best, and perhaps even depressing . . . if not for the reader, certainly for the author.

PART 1

The Soul Under Siege

CHAPTER 1

An Outline of Temptation

T HE APOSTLE JOHN warned his fellow Christians about the mortal danger of friendship with the world. "Do not love the world," he wrote, "nor the things in the world." In fact, John went on, "If anyone loves the world, the love of the Father is not in him" (1 John 2:15).

In this text "the world" is understood in a sense very different from its use in John 3:16, "God so loved the world." When John says here, "Do not love the world," he means the world in its fallen and rebellious state, described by St. Paul as "subjected to futility" and in "the bondage of corruption" (Rom. 8:20–21). This is the world of which Jesus declares, "because you are not of the world, but I chose you out of the world, therefore the world hates you" (John 15:19). This is the world for which Jesus declined to pray (John 17:9).

In the "world" that John tells us not to love, there are only three things: "the lust of the flesh, the lust of the eyes, and the pride of life" (1 John 2:16). The world here described is the world alienated from God by the Fall of our first parents.

Indeed, in the Bible's description of Eve's initial act of disobedience, we may discern these three identical elements: "the lust of the flesh, the lust of the eyes, and the pride of life." Describing the defection of Eve, Holy Scripture says, "So when the woman saw that the tree was good for food [the lust of the flesh], that it was pleasant to the eyes [the lust of the eyes], and a tree desirable to make one wise [the pride of life], she took of its fruit and ate" (Gen. 3:6).

Probably because she was the world's first offender, Holy Scripture goes into some detail to describe the temptation to which Eve succumbed. An outline of her temptation serving as a kind of paradigm of all temptation, Eve stands as the Bible's first negative model of the moral life; her lapse provides the initial description of how the demons deal with the human soul.

Perhaps, moreover, St. Paul was indicating as much when he wrote to the church at Corinth, "I fear, lest somehow, as the serpent deceived Eve by his crafti- ness, so your minds may be corrupted from the sim- plicity that is in Christ" (2 Cor. 11:3). Thus, if we want to understand how temptation functions in human psychology, we can hardly do better than to examine the temptation of Eve.

At each stage in the triple temptation, Eve indulges a specious reasoning begotten of her passions. Objec- tive moral strictures are not consulted. Eve's fall results from a distorted pattern of reasoning, for her thoughts are dictated by her desires.

And how did Eve stumble into this tripartite temptation? By giving ear to the deceptive argu- ments of the Serpent. The latter begins with a factual question: "Has God indeed said, 'You shall not eat of every tree of the garden'?" (Gen. 3:1). The idea is preposterous, and Eve hastens to correct the ques- tioner. She feels justified in this, of course, because in answering the Serpent she can even feel herself to be God's defender. Alas, however, a conversation with the Deceiver has therewith begun, and fickle Eve is a poor match for him. Her first mistake, then, was tac- tical. She should never have answered him at all.

Eve's mind now engaged, the Deceiver prompts her to question the very reason that God had given for the command, "for in the day that you eat of it, you shall surely die" (Gen. 2:17). In fact, Eve had never heard God say these words, for they were spoken before she was formed from Adam's rib. Eve knew of the prohibition only through Adam.

That is to say, God's mandate, as far as Eve knew, was simply a moral tradition, perhaps subject to improvement. Why need she submit her moral judgment to the apodictic command that Adam had shared with her? She, after all, had a mind of her own. She was just as intelligent as Adam, who after all had not really been in this world much longer than she. She could figure things out for herself. Thus did our ancient mother commence the process of her own personal moral theory.

Saint Paul describes Eve's beguilement as a corruption from "simplicity" (2 Cor. 11:3). In place of God's emphatic command, known solely through the moral tradition available to her, Eve declared the autonomy of her own thought, not pausing to consider that her thinking was nothing more than the perverse assertion of her passions.

CHAPTER 2

Lurking Thought

G ENESIS DOES NOT say why God rejected Cain's sacrifice while accepting that of Abel. The answer to that question is intimated, however, in Hebrews 11:4: "By faith Abel offered to God a more excellent sacrifice than Cain, through which he obtained witness that he was righteous, God testifying of his gifts." Cain, we are given to understand, was deficient in faith, so he could not please God because "without faith it is impossible to please Him" (11:6).

Lacking faith, Cain was likewise wanting in insight with respect to his real spiritual state. Cain was under attack and did not know it. God warned him that evil was "lurking at the door" (Gen 4:7). The Hebrew participle for "lurking" here, *robesh*, can also be rendered as "crouching." It is the posture of a pred-atory animal about to pounce.

Rabash, the root verb of this Hebrew participle, is related to the name of a wily spirit known as Rabishu in Assyro-Babylonian literature; he is pictured as crouch-ing along the road, endeavoring to waylay the traveler. Temptation was portrayed, then, as lying in wait for a man, stalking him, as it were, and Cain was exhorted to vigilance, lest he be taken down. Thus, Cain was warned not to fool with temptation; it is dangerous.

Cain's mother Eve, after all, had made the big mis-take of dialoguing with the Snake. Satan invariably conquers those who discuss things with him. Or, as we read in Sirach 21:2, "Flee from sin as from the face of a serpent, for if you come too near to it, it will bite you."

Cain gave no heed to the divine warning, none-theless, and went on to kill his brother (Gen. 4:8–10). Thus, the original sin of the parents in Genesis 3 led directly to the sin of the child in Genesis 4. The jeal-ousy and violence of Cain were the proper products of that original act of infidelity. The first human being begotten of human parents was also the first murderer.

Cain's murder was not a crime of passion. It came, rather, at the end of a slower spiritual deteriora-tion. Lacking faith, the sinner began by hardening his mind against God. "Am I my brother's keeper?" (Gen. 4:9), Cain haughtily inquired of the Almighty, demonstrating by this irreverence that he had closed off his conscience. This disrespect for God was the foundation on which his murder was based. Cain would not have killed had he not isolated his spirit from the divine light and voice.

Moreover, by this murder Cain alienated himself from the very earth on which he walked: "So now you are cursed from the earth, which has opened its mouth to receive your brother's blood from your hand. When you till the ground, it will no longer yield its strength to you. A fugitive and a vagabond you will be on the earth" (Gen. 4:11–12).

Cain had begun as a farmer, but now he was estranged even from the soil. He assumed, by his sin, the contradictory task of being a wandering farmer. However, the foundational reason for Cain's alienation from the earth and his fellow men was his alienation from God: "Cain went out from the presence of the Lord" (Gen. 4:16).

And, because violence breeds vengeance, this was not the end of Cain's story. He became afraid of the retaliation that might be visited on his head because of his murder of Abel (Gen. 4:14). Ironically, God's reply, though reassuring to Cain himself, extended yet further the domain of violence: "Whoever kills Cain, vengeance will be taken on him sevenfold" (4:15).

Such was the context of the world's first city (Gen. 4:17), Enoch, which was founded by Cain. Yes, this first great effort of social cooperation was inaugurated by a murderer!

The first city was founded, moreover, by the first fratricide, a fact that became the most ironical of archetypes. Its irony was certainly not lost on St. Augustine, who commented at some length on the manifest travesty that such a great enterprise of brotherly cooperation should be undertaken by a man that killed his brother. In his lengthy *The City of God*, the saintly bishop of Hippo compared Cain's founding of the city of Enoch to the founding of the city of Rome by Romulus, who also had killed his own brother, Remus.

Sinful man's attempt to build, that is to say, uses the very components of deterioration. Cain's original failure of faith lay at the heart of the problem. Merely human exertions do not improve man's true plight; at best, they but disguise it for a while. The heart of all evil is unbelief and alienation from God, so a society thus established has already drunk the poison. Like Adam and Eve, it will surely die.

CHAPTER 3

Impulsive Gratification

T HOUGH HIS APPEARANCE in history was, I suppose, a bit too early to warrant the term, *modern man* seems an apt expression for the biblical character Esau. At least we can call him modern in one large and defining sense: Esau, for the sole purpose of gratifying an immediate impulse, thoughtlessly betrayed an inherited treasure. The New Testament, in its only complaint against him, describes Esau as a "profane person . . . who for one morsel of food sold his birthright" (Heb. 12:16).

First, Esau's underlying weakness was a lack of elementary self-control. As a rugged outdoorsman (Gen. 25:27), perhaps he thought of himself as a man of tough discipline. Clearly, however, the very opposite was true. Esau was unable to control his appetite even long enough for a meal to be prepared for him. Like a nursing infant, he insisted on being fed *right now*, as though he would otherwise perish: "Look, I am about to die; so what is this birthright to me?" (25:32) Undisciplined Esau, that is to say, gave up his inheritance for a slight but instant gratification, and this is the first and radical reason why I call him a modern man.

Esau was also modern in a second way, in that he had no real sense of the relative worth of things. Because he had cheaply sold something material, he assumed that he could just as cheaply purchase something spiritual. Embracing the principle that man lives by bread alone, he nonetheless fancied that a higher benediction was still available to him, pretty much at the same price. Having lost his birthright for a bowl of soup, he planned to gain his blessing with a plate of venison.

There is a third display of Esau's modernity: He was slow to learn that the future is very much tied to the past. Some blessings—and among them the very best—are inseparable from birthrights, so that the reckless squandering of the one renders unlikely the acquisition of the other. Those, therefore, who contemn the past have little chance for a future. Poor Esau! The

New Testament describes his plight: "For you know that afterward, when he wanted to inherit the blessing, he was rejected, for he found no place for repentance, though he sought it diligently with tears" (Heb. 12:17).

There is a fourth sense in which Esau appears as a modern man—the willful assertion of his individuality at the expense of his personhood. Persons, after all, are defined by their relationships to others, especially others in the past. Indeed, persons receive their very names from those who arrived in this world before them. There is no personhood without community and tradition, because persons are created when someone else, someone older, tells us who we are.

Persons, thus, are necessarily formed within the context of an eldership; a person is someone who stands under the authority of what Ken Myers of *Mars Hill Audio* has called "a community of binding address," in which those who go before have authority over those who come after. Personhood, therefore, requires a living tradition and a committed acquiescence in the authority of elders.

An individual is something quite different. His relations to others do not define him. He is, on the contrary, very much self-defined. He is someone distinct from others. The Bible required but few words to tell the trait of the individualist: "Thus, Esau despised his birthright" (Gen. 25:34). An individual is a self-made man. He does not derive who he is as a free and generous bequest from the past; he acquires it by his independence and self-determination in the present.

In these various ways of describing him as modern, I have in mind chiefly Esau's deliberate alienation from what could and should have been his own, and what he could and should have been able to bequeath to his posterity. His sin consisted in separating himself from tradition, the transmission of an intergenerational inheritance.

The character of Esau goes far to illustrate post-cultural man, a term coined by Christopher Clausen in his book *Faded Mosaic* in 2000; the term serves to identify the deeply isolated individual deprived of the wealth and wisdom of a living heritage. Emancipated from answering to the authority of the past, this post-cultural man is necessarily deprived of a fully human community in the present. He belongs only to the "now," reduced to a spiritually meager, less-than-human cohabitation in what sociologist Robert Bellah calls a "lifestyle enclave" (*Habits of the Heart: Individualism and Commitment in American Life*). Poor Esau, coming from nowhere, now lives nowhere, and has nowhere to go.

CHAPTER 4

The Love of the World

D URING THE TWO years that the Apostle Paul spent in prison at Caesarea (Acts 24:27), certain of his fellow workers had sufficient access to him that he could include them with the note "sends greetings" in the epistles that he wrote at that time. Their number included his "fellow laborers," Mark, Aristarchus, Demas, and Luke (Phil. 1:24).

It is curious, as we shall see, that Paul mentions Demas and Luke together. Near the end of the Epistle to the Colossians (4:14), composed during the same period, Paul wrote, "Luke the beloved physician and Demas greet you."

It appears that these two men, Demas and Luke, afterward traveled with Paul to Rome, where he spent another two years under house arrest (Acts 28:30). When, writing to Timothy toward the end of that time, Paul was preparing to die, and he made one final and very significant reference to Demas and Luke: "Demas has forsaken me, having loved this present world, and has departed for Thessaloniki. . . . Only Luke is with me" (2 Tim. 4:10–11).

We know a good deal about the rest of Luke's career, of course, but about Demas we hear not another word, nor does this final reference prompt us much to hope for him—"having loved this present world."

Demas had his chance, so to speak. Had he not loved "this present world" (literally, "the now age"— *to nun aiona*), there is every reason to suspect that he would be invoked throughout Christian history as St. Demas and, like Luke, be remembered with a feast day in the Christian calendar.

So what happened? Demas loved "the present age," we are told. That is to say, through all his time of ministry, even sharing in some measure the apostolic hardships of St. Paul, Demas remained at root a worldly man. Mark, another of his friends, described folks of this sort, in whom "the cares of the world [*tou aionos*], the deceitfulness of riches, and the desires for other things entering in choke the word, and it becomes unfruitful" (Mark 4:19).

Surely it was not the case that Demas, St. Paul's fellow worker, had never been cautioned about worldliness. Is it possible to think he had not once heard Paul admonish, "do not be conformed to this world [*to aioni touto*]" (Rom. 12:2)? How could any companion of the Apostle Paul be ignorant about the perils of "the world" or "the present age" (1 Cor. 1:20; 2:6, 8; 3:18; 2 Cor. 4:4; Gal. 1:4; Eph. 1:21; 6:12; Titus 2:12 [*en to nun aioni*]).

Nor was this pessimism concerning the world a peculiarity of Paul. The Apostle John, though he does not use Paul's expression *aion* to speak of it, often employs the noun *kosmos* in pretty much the same moral sense—namely, the "world" as creation in rebellion against God. This was the world for which Jesus refused to pray (John 17:9), the world out of which the Lord called His disciples that they should not belong to it (17:6, 11), the world that hates both Him and them (15:18, 19; 17:14; 1 John 3:1, 13; 4:17).

The failure of Demas was that he loved the world. It is remarkable that Paul should use the participle *agapesas* in reference to Demas's love of the world, because normally this verb refers to God's love for men, men's love for God, and their love of one another in God. However unusual, nonetheless, this is the same verb employed by St. John when he warns

Christians, "Do not love the world [*me agapate ton kosmon*] or the things in the world" (1 John 2:15).

The context of this passage throws a helpful light on the tragedy of Demas, for John goes on to comment, "If anyone loves the world, the love of the Father is not in him." The world does not know God and cannot receive the Holy Spirit (John 14:7). There is an absolute gulf, therefore, between the world and the Father. We suspect that Demas did not see this right away, because a man does not suddenly go from complete fidelity to total loss of faith. The decline is usually by degrees.

Toward the end, however, and perhaps after years of compromising, Demas himself came to see that God and the world constitute a decisive either/or, because "all that *is* in the world—the lust of the flesh, the lust of the eyes, and the pride of life—is not of the Father but is of the world" (1 John 2:16). One cannot forever have it both ways. Faced with this radical either/or, worldly Demas made his choice.

CHAPTER 5

Caution and the Sacred

ONE OF THE stories that has proved troubling to students of Holy Scripture over the years is the account of Uzzah, who stretched forth his hand to steady the Ark of the Covenant. The Ark, we recall, was being carried by oxcart in order to be installed at David's projected new shrine at Jerusalem. Some obstacle, however, perhaps a bump in the road, caused the oxen to lurch, nearly upsetting the cart and putting the Ark in danger. The Bible describes the scene: "Uzzah put out his hand to the Ark of God and took hold of it, for the oxen stumbled. Then the anger of the Lord was aroused against Uzzah, and God struck him there for his error; and he died there by the Ark of God" (2 Sam. 6:6–7).

The shock of readers is surely understandable. Wasn't Uzzah's sudden reaction, after all, simply an instinctive response to save the dignity of the Ark? To the extent that we can even describe his deed as intentional, wasn't that intention good and honorable? How is it, then, that the all-seeing Lord, the God who searches hearts, did not look favorably on what Uzzah did? Shouldn't he have been rewarded rather than punished?

The problem is not a recent one, and readers of the Bible have pondered it for centuries. For example, the Jewish historian Josephus, writing about the same time as some New Testament authors, explained that Uzzah was struck dead for touching the Ark, "since he was not a priest" (*me on hierus*) (*Antiquities of the Jews, 7.4.2.81*). This explanation of Josephus is based on prescriptions in Numbers 4, which lists the duties of priests and Levites in regard to the treatment and transportation of the Ark.

This interpretation of the event, which does not necessarily imply a conscious moral failing on the part of Uzzah, is essentially sound, I believe. The Ark of God was very holy, and holiness is dangerous. Uzzah was killed when he touched something holy.

In this respect it is important to reflect how little we know about the *divina*, the things of God. The little we do know will prompt us, surely, to be cautious in how we handle them, even in our minds.

The things of God are not what we want or imagine them to be. God Himself determines what they are, and God has not the slightest concern for our own interpretations of them. Their holiness is definite, real, and even physical.

Holiness is likewise not dependent on man's recognition of it. It resembles electricity in this respect. The trespasser who is electrocuted when climbing too high on a high-voltage tower perishes without regard to his own understanding of what he is about, or his innocent intentions, or his personal theories concerning electricity.

That is to say, the things of God are not safe.

David learned this lesson about holiness from the death of Uzzah. Consequently, when the Ark was later returned to Jerusalem, it was borne, not by oxcart, but on the shoulders of the Levites, as it was supposed to be and as God had prescribed (1 Chron. 15:2, 15; Deut. 10:8; 31:25; 1 Sam. 6:15).

David perceived what must be perceived by any who would approach the living God in worship— God decides the nature, structure, and spirit of the worship. Our religious feelings—whether by private or corporate preference—do not determine how we worship. The content and form of our worship has been established, rather, by the inherited, authoritative transmission of the worship itself. We hand it on as we have received it. We do not take it upon ourselves to give form to the worship. If we are faithful, the worship gives form to us, and the example of Uzzah instructs us on the peril of acting otherwise.

Correct (orthodox) worship is not the uninformed, spontaneous outpouring of human activity, and the worshipper must be on guard against identifying his personal impulses with the agency of the Holy Spirit. Undisciplined, off-the-cuff people are far more likely to act under the impulse of suspect and impure spirits than under the guidance of the Holy Spirit. For this reason, mere spontaneity and a sense of fulfillment in worship are not adequate nor reliable indications of the agency of the Holy Spirit.

David perceived that correct worship is not chiefly concerned with meeting the religious needs and aspirations of human beings, but with the glory of God, which is inseparable from His holiness. The fundamental ground of true worship is not the religious nature of man, but the glorious manifestation of God. Indeed, any worship that is not a response to God's self-revelation must of necessity be idolatrous, the worship of something that man himself creates from the resources of his own religious nature.

For worship to be authentic and true, therefore, God Himself takes the initiative. God must be revealed in order for man to worship correctly, and God determines how He is to be worshipped. Otherwise, man is simply worshipping the works of his own hands, the thoughts of his own mind. Orthodox worship does not consist in the attempt to express man's religious aspirations, but in meeting, in faith, the manifestation of God in His truth. If man thinks to worship God without rules and rubrics, heaven only knows what he is up to.

CHAPTER 6

Coming Undone

HISTORY ABOUNDS IN stories of men that showed great promise in their youth but ended their days in utter ruin. Some of these were laid low by events and conditions beyond their control, to be sure, but the downfall of others seems to have come from some personal flaw, some deep spiritual defect that ate away the content of their character and brought them to a bitter end. In the latter category no example, perhaps, lives so vividly in memory as old King Saul.

Who can forget young Saul's sudden, dramatic appearance on the stage of history? It was about 1020 BC that Nahash, the king of Ammon, laid siege to the Israelite town of Jabesh-Gilead, close to the

Ammonite border. The citizens of Jabesh, thinking that Nahash wanted only an annual tribute for his treasury, promptly offered to comply. The Ammonites, however, had something more in mind. Apparently still chafing under their humiliating defeat by Jephthah a few generations earlier, these invaders determined to seek reprisal by subjecting the citizens of Jabesh to a special punishment, bringing all Israel to disgrace. In the words of Nahash, "On this condition I will make a covenant with you, that I may put out all your right eyes, and bring reproach on all Israel" (1 Sam. 11:2).

So much for international diplomacy.

Delegates were dispatched from Jabesh to see if anyone in the rest of Israel would come to their aid, and in due course these delegates found their way to the city of Gibeah. They arrived just about the time that young Saul was coming in from plowing his fields.

What we see next is a good illustration of Saul's personality and justifies our describing him as a strong executive type, blessed with a high energy level: "So he took a yoke of oxen and cut them in pieces, and sent them throughout all the territory of Israel by the hands of messengers, saying, 'Whoever does not go out with Saul and Samuel to battle, so it shall be done to his oxen'" (1 Sam. 11:7).

This challenge, coming from a powerful man described as "taller than any of the people from his shoulder upward" (1 Sam. 10:23), elicited the desired response: "And the fear of the Lord fell on the people, and they came out with one consent" (11:7). The siege of Jabesh was quickly relieved, Nahash's Ammonites were sent packing, and no one in Israel was in doubt about who was in charge.

History obliges us to contrast this glorious entrance of Saul with the pathetic figure of the king's later years, when he suffered from periods of debilitating depression (1 Sam. 16:14), uncontrolled jealousy (18:8), mindless suspicions (20:30), and a paranoia so severe that he was obliged to sit with his back to the wall (20:25). Most pathetic of all, perhaps, was Saul's recourse to a sorceress on the very night before he fell on his sword, defeated at the Battle of Mount Gilboah (28:3–25; 31:1–4).

When we look for a cause of the downfall of Saul, we recognize that the king was laid low by the very qualities of his personality that had brought him to the throne. Saul began as a man of swift, executive decision-making, with a high energy level. He was blessed with those traits, and he continued to develop them . . . until they destroyed him.

Men of that type, unless someone warns them of the attendant dangers, may be disposed to cultivate those features beyond any useful purpose. They may fail, therefore, to develop other virtues to complement and refine the native merits of their type. These virtues include elements difficult for quick, executive decision-makers, such as patience, humility, and the habit of objective reflection.

And here is where Saul came to grief. His recorded failures involved his assumption of an executive authority he did not have. This assumption is clear in his impatient effort to take on the service of a priest (1 Sam. 13:1–14), his reckless disobedience in the matter of the Amalekites (15:1–19), and his endeavor to enforce a rash oath (14:33–45). Finally, it led him to the cold-blooded murder of the priests of Nob (22:6–19).

The downfall of Saul stands forever as a warning against playing relentlessly to one's strengths, especially if those strengths encourage impatience and the temptation to self-glorification. In the case of Saul, these very strengths turned him into the morbid, vengeful, superstitious old man who perished on the heights of Gilboah.

PART 2

Frailty and Betrayal

CHAPTER 7

The Undisciplined Eye

ABIMELECH, THE KING of Gerar, had an appreciative eye for handsome women. True, this trait brought him briefly to grief on one occasion, but they say he learned from the experience.

The incident began when some newcomers, Abraham and Sarah, settled in the neighborhood. When Sarah was introduced as Abraham's sister, poor Abimelech at one glance felt himself going all gooey inside. At the sight of this beautiful, apparently unmarried woman, the king's ardently smitten heart started to flutter like a leaf in the breeze. With a single look at the lady (a look that sober minds may have judged injudiciously long), Abimelech found his knees shaky and his throat dry. This lovely Sarah was surely meant for him, the king had no doubt.

And, being the king, Abimelech was accustomed to getting what he wanted. Indeed, royal courting and romancing were rather uncomplicated in those days; Abimelech simply sent over to Abraham's place and had Sarah removed to the royal palace. It all happened very fast. In fact, the story so far is contained in just one Bible verse (Gen. 20:2).

Now in the considerations that follow, let us be temperate with Abimelech. He was, after all, a man in love, and men thus stricken have been known to act precipitously once in a while. The king was lovesick. Let us be gentle with him.

Nonetheless, let us also be frank. Abimelech should have known that this was not a smart move. Certain features of the case, if he had thought on them, might have prompted the king to a greater and more salutary caution.

Not least among these was the fact that lovely Sarah was ninety years old at the time (Gen. 17:17), and Abimelech should have given that circumstance the reflection it deserved. This was not good. Please understand, the abrupt abduction of a ninety-year-old woman for amorous purposes is in very bad form. Among gentlemen, at least, it simply isn't done. And when it is done, let me tell you, most of the time the thing doesn't work out.

Second, Abimelech was wrong to take at face value the assertion, "She is my sister." That was one of Abraham's old tricks to avoid getting his throat slit by other men who, it appears, were forever falling in love with his unusually attractive wife. Years before, for instance, when he and Sarah were visiting Egypt, the pharaoh down there had been similarly smitten with her. Not only had Abraham on that occasion saved his own life by recourse to his she-is-my-sister routine, but also the pharaoh gave Abraham lots of nice presents to honor him. Then, when the whole thing blew up in the pharaoh's face, Abraham still got to keep the presents (Gen. 12:11–20). That is to say, the ruse paid off.

Abraham, if questioned further about Sarah's being his sister, could always point out that *sister* in Hebrew really means "female relative," and Sarah was a blood relative—his half sister, in fact (Gen. 20:12). Obviously this convenient arrangement was useful for throwing would-be rivals into confusion, nor did Abraham scruple much on the matter. Although we are never told Sarah's views about it, we do know that she tended to appreciate the humor and irony of things (18:11–12).

Anyway, to return to our story, Abimelech thought Sarah definitely the woman of his dreams. These dreams, however, began turning sour right away: "But God came to Abimelech in a dream by night, and said to him, 'Indeed, you are a dead man because the woman you have taken is a man's wife'" (Gen. 20:3). Abimelech argued his innocence, a point the Lord conceded, and in the morning Sarah was returned, untouched, to her husband. Both of them were rebuked for the deception, but Abimelech still loaded them down with more presents (20:4–16).

As I remarked earlier, Abimelech learned from the experience. Some years later Isaac, the son of Abraham and Sarah, came to settle at Gerar with his beautiful wife, Rebekah. Once again, sure enough, Isaac tried to pass Rebekah off as his sister; she was, in fact, a cousin. This time, however, chary Abimelech did not bite. He simply kept a watchful eye on the couple, until one day he "looked through a window, and saw, and there was Isaac showing endearment to Rebekah his wife" (Gen. 26:6–8). *Aha, I knew it,* thought the king to himself, *you just can't be too careful these days.*

CHAPTER 8

All in Perspective

F EW STATEMENTS, I confess, render my mind more uneasy than the simple declaration, "Well, it all depends on how you look at it." When I hear this sentence, a sudden, anxious impulse at the back of the brain sends out the general warning, *Caution! You are about to hear something unbelievably stupid.*

This response on my part is not natural, of course, in the sense of being a thing of nature. Such a reaction is hardly to be explained by the genes. No, mine is a truly conditioned reflex, produced by years of monotonous reruns of nonsense. After about the millionth time of hearing someone say, "It all depends on how you look at it," followed immediately by something unbelievably idiotic, the conditioned memory simply links the two things together as components of a whole.

Not only is my reaction not natural, it is also not rational. That is to say, there is no logical or necessary connection between statements of unbelievable stupidity and the affirmation "it all depends on how you look at it." The two things are connected only in my experience.

Moreover, not only is my reaction not natural and not logical, sometimes it is also unwarranted. It is a fact that many things in life depend entirely on "how you look at it." For instance, the famous Mediterranean cloud that Elijah beheld from Mount Carmel was not really the size of a man's hand. It was a great deal larger, or Elijah could not have seen it. Making the cloud the size of a man's hand depended entirely on "how you look at it." The relative size of Elijah's cloud truly was a matter of perspective.

Phidias, likewise, demonstrated this sense of perspective very well in his design of the Parthenon. When we visitors climb through the entrance to the Acropolis at Athens, we look across toward the Parthenon on the other side, and we see a building that appears to be perfectly symmetric. (Indeed, unless we deliberately advert to the fact, we may not even notice that we are looking at the Parthenon at an angle, not straight on. Phidias had no intention of our looking at it straight on.) From our perspective on the opposite side of the Acropolis, all the columns supporting the Parthenon appear to be the same size. That is the way Phidias designed it to be seen.

When we walk over and inspect the building more closely, however, it looks very different. The columns are of very different sizes. They appear to be the same size only when viewed from the vectored perspective at the entrance to the Acropolis. This is simply art, and in art it is undeniably true that "it all depends on how you look at it."

Why, then, do I react so unnaturally and illogically to unqualified declarations that "it all depends on how you look at it"? As I indicated above, it comes from a burdened memory. "It all depends on how you look at it" has become, in my experience, an all-purpose antecedent from which nearly any conclusion, no matter how unbelievable, can be drawn.

As I have heard the expression, "it all depends on how you look at it" most often means, "There is no such thing as truth; everything is point of view." Or, "we cannot know reality; we can only tell our stories." There is nothing beyond interpretation. Truth is nothing so rock solid as the Parthenon. The only reality is personal or corporate narrative. Even if truth exists, we cannot know it, because every perspective is angled from a personal vantage or shared point of view.

Although this absolutist claim for perspective is so modern as to be postmodern, it is not without its precedents in the past. Among the ancients who contended, as a point of dogma, that "it all depends on how you look at it" was King Balak of Moab. This monarch combined a boundless confidence in the power of perspective with a dogged determination, no matter what the cost, to get the angle just so. Balak knew exactly what he wanted to be seen, and he was persuaded that it would surely be seen, if only he could arrange the proper point of view.

This is the spirit behind Balak's pathetic attempts to make Balaam look at Israel's army just so. Three times he insists that Balaam stand here or stand there, on each occasion gaining a different viewpoint. Balak knows what he wants Balaam to behold and, if he can get Balaam standing in exactly the right place, he will behold it (Num. 23:3, 13, 27). After all, truth, as everyone knows, enjoys no independent existence. It all depends on how you look at it.

Balak's effort doesn't work, of course. Poor, disappointing Balaam keeps seeing what he sees. No matter which direction he turns, before him stand the awesome, invincible forces of Israel still holding the field, utterly undeniable, powerful as the Parthenon. No slanting of the story, no contrived vectoring of the light, can vanquish the irreducible claims of the truth, and at last Balak pleads with Balaam to break it off, please, and go home (Num. 24:10–11). Truth can never be reduced to perspective.

CHAPTER 9

Enticement

A MONG THE STORIES in Genesis more easily remembered—even if only for being a bit
racy—is the one about Joseph's temptation by Potiphar's wife (39:7–20). When the young man told
her, "Oh no, ma'am, this is a really bad idea," the lady
took the rejection personally, as they say, and went
on to accuse Joseph of trying to seduce *her.* Joseph
then was thrown in jail, until "the king sent and
released him, the ruler of the people let him go free"
(Ps. 104/105:20).

The tale of Joseph and Potiphar's wife was not
antiquity's sole narrative of a young man falsely
accused by a married woman after resisting her adul-
terous enticements. An Egyptian manuscript, for

example, closely dated to about 1225 BC (*Papyrus D'Orbiney*, British Museum, 10183), records a strikingly similar story of two brothers and the wife of the older brother.

In this account, the younger brother, Bata, lived in the home of the older, Anubis, as a sort of dependent, who did all the work on the farm. As Bata grew to full manhood, the wife of Anubis began to cast on this younger brother an ever more lustful eye. Like Joseph, Bata was physically attractive. Indeed, the text says, "There was no one like him in the entire land. Why, the strength of a god was in him." The wife of Anubis endeavored to seduce Bata, but he steadfastly resisted her allurements. Outraged at being thus scorned, she accused him of attempted rape. Anubis, of course, believed her.

The several similarities between this tale and the Joseph story are all the more striking inasmuch as both accounts come from the same time (late second millennium BC) and place (Egypt).

The theme was hardly limited to Egypt, however. Homer told an almost identical story of "peerless Bellerophon," to whom "the gods granted beauty and manly appeal." The wife of Proteus, lovely Anteia, longed with mad passion to lie in secret love with Bellerophon. Her efforts, however, were wasted on "wise

Bellerophon, who discerned what was proper" (*Iliad*, 6.150–168). Like Mrs. Potiphar, Anteia then accused the young man of attempting to seduce her, and Proteus, like Potiphar, believed his wife.

This pattern is found repeatedly in classical literature. Thus, Apollodorus tells the tale of young Peleus, who was indicted by Cretheis, the wife of Acastus, when he declined her advances. Pausanias similarly tells of the wife of Crethesus, Biadice, who lusted after handsome Phrixus and, when he rebuffed her, mendaciously accused him. Both Apollodorus and Pausanias write of Tenes, who was tempted by Philonome, the wife of Cycnus. When the young man withstood her charms, Philonome retaliated by charging him with attempted rape.

Again Ovid and others tell the story of Hippolytus, against whom Phaedra, the wife of Theseus, brought the same accusation after her unsuccessful attempt at seduction.

Within the common pattern of all these stories, the names themselves are nearly interchangeable. There is invariably an innocent, young, unmarried man—call him Joseph, Bata, Peleus, or whatever—who unwittingly catches the roaming eye of an older, more experienced, married woman. She, endeavoring to seduce the young fellow, is scorned, and in revenge she falsely accuses *him* of being the offender.

Although most of these stories are preserved in mythology where they do not serve an explicitly moral purpose, they can all certainly be read for that purpose, and the moral lesson thus derived is identical in each. Namely, a young man receives the very sound counsel that he must "flee from the flattering tongue of a seductress" (Prov. 6:24). This is a very old theme in Wisdom literature. An ancient Akkadian text (*A Pessimistic Dialogue Between Master and Servant*) refers to such a woman as "a sharp iron dagger that cuts a man's neck." In cases like this, mere exhortations to chastity are not enough. What is required is swift and decisive flight.

In the story of Joseph, the theme of Wisdom is explicit and pronounced (Gen. 41:39; Ps. 104/105:22), and here Potiphar's wife serves as the very incarnation of Dame Folly, that quintessential adventuress trying to seduce the inexperienced young man (Prov. 2:16; 5:2–6, 20; 6:24–35; 7:5). As Joseph learned to his considerable hurt, it was in reference to Potiphar's wife and residence that the wise man was warned, "Remove your way far from her, / And do not go near the door of her house" (5:8).

CHAPTER 10

Youthful Folly

REHOBOAM WAS ALMOST the perfect example of what the Bible means by the word *fool*. Because he was the son of Solomon, Israel's wisest king, furthermore, this foolishness was a matter of irony as well as tragedy.

After Solomon's death in 922, this heir to Israel's throne traveled to Schechem to receive the nation's endorsement as its new ruler. The move was especially necessary with respect to Israel's northern tribes, a people touchy about their traditional rights and needing to be handled gently. Even David, we recall, had to be made king twice, first over Judah about the year 1000 (2 Sam. 2:4, 10) and then over the north some years later (5:4–5).

Those northern tribes, for their part, seemed willing to be ruled by Rehoboam, but they craved assurance that the new king would respect their ancient traditions and customs. Truth be told, they had not been entirely happy with Rehoboam's father, Solomon, and they sought from his son a simple pledge that their grievances would be taken seriously in the future (1 Kin. 12:1–4). A great deal depended on Rehoboam's answer.

The new king apparently took the matter seriously, because he sought counsel on what to say. He began by consulting the seniors of the royal court, the very men who had for forty years provided guidance for his father. These were the elder statesmen of the realm, those qualified to give the most prudent political counsel.

Significantly, these older men urged Rehoboam in the direction of caution and moderation with respect to the northern tribes: "If you will be a servant to this people today and serve them, and speak good words to them when you answer them, then they will be your servants forever" (1 Kin. 12:7).

Rehoboam, nonetheless, eschewing the instruction of his elders, followed the impulses of his younger companions, who encouraged him to stand tough and not let himself be pushed around. Indeed,

they urged Rehoboam to be insulting and provoca-
tive to the petitioners (1 Kin. 12:8–11). Pursuing this
foolish counsel, then, he immediately lost the larger
part of his kingdom (12:12–16).

As I suggested above, there is great irony here, for
it may be said that one of the major practical purposes of the Book of Proverbs, traditionally ascribed
to Solomon, was to prevent and preclude exactly the
mistake made by Solomon's son. According to Proverbs, the fool is the man who ignores the counsel of
the old and follows the impulses of untried youth.

Many a life has been ruined—and in this case,
a kingdom lost—because someone preferred the
pooled stupidity of his contemporaries to the accu-
mulated wisdom of his elders. Those whose counsel
Rehoboam spurned, after all, were not just any old
men. They were the very ancients who had provided
guidance to Israel's most sagacious monarch.

Rehoboam's reign of seventeen years knew its ups
and downs, the downs dominant. Five years after the
story narrated above, Pharaoh Shishak invaded the
Holy Land and took pretty much whatever attracted
his eye: "In the fifth year of King Rehoboam,
Shishak king of Egypt came up against Jerusalem.
He took away the treasures of the house of the Lord
and the treasures of the king's house. He took away

everything. He also took away all the shields of gold that Solomon had made" (1 Kin. 14:26).

The sacred text goes on to remark, "King Rehoboam made in their place shields of bronze" (1 Kin. 14:27). By setting bronze shields in the Temple to replace the golden shields of Solomon, Rehoboam enacted a truly wretched symbolism. Some of the ancients (Daniel, Hesiod, Ovid) spoke of an historical decline from a golden age to a silver age, and thence to a bronze age. No one disputes, of course, that Solomon's was a golden age (10:14–29). However, the reign of Rehoboam, his heir, was not just a declension to silver, but all the way to bronze. The lunge, when it came, came at once, in a single generation.

Rehoboam remained, Josephus tells us, "a proud and foolish man" (*Antiquities of the Jews,* 8.10.4). He never recovered from the singular folly of his first political decision. After Shishak's invasion, this thin, pathetic shadow of his father and grandfather reigned under a humiliating Egyptian suzerainty for a dozen more years. Like every fool, he had a heart problem. The final word about Rehoboam asserts, "he did evil, for he did not set his heart to seek the Lord" (2 Chron. 12:14).

CHAPTER 11

The Shallow Heart

I F SHE WAS even half as pretty as Hedy Lamarr, who played her in Cecil B. DeMille's 1949 film, it is easy to see why Samson was fascinated with Delilah.

Fascinated too, over the centuries, were those many readers of Holy Scripture who found in the tragic romance of Delilah and the Danite judge the stuff of (as Milton remarks on the subject in his poem "Samson Agonistes") "Acts enroll'd/ In copious Legend, or sweet Lyric Song."

However, the romance, it would seem, was mainly on Samson's side. While the Bible asserts that he loved Delilah (Judg. 16:4), it does not even faintly hint that she loved him.

Much less do the pair appear to have been married. Milton's "Samson Agonistes" is an exception in regarding them as such, though Chaucer (in "The Monk's Tale") does extract from their dolorous story a practical if dubious domestic counsel—namely, that wives are not to be trusted in matters touching limb and life.

The Delilah of DeMille's film is a Philistine, and this construction of the story is common. Indeed, Sainte-Saën's opera on the theme portrays her as an ardent nationalist, eager to avenge the Philistines' humiliation at Samson's hand.

Curiously, the portrayal of Delilah as a Philistine patriot makes her a mirror image, as it were, of Judith, who employed her native charms to wile the heart and whack off the head of Holofernes. We see them differently, nonetheless. The exploit we applaud in the daughter of Merari we deplore in the lady from Sorek Valley. The biblical Delilah, that is to say, is scarcely a winning figure.

DeMille did his best to make her such, not only by enhancing her with the merits of Hedy Lamarr, but by introducing into her heart a genuine affection of Samson. The loyalty of this affection is tested in the story, a trial that fills Delilah with uncertainty and moral angst. Indeed, DeMille transforms her into a tragic figure, a sort of female Samson and his very counterpart, tossed about with doubts and torn with inner conflicts. Like Samson, she too repents at the end. One would think they were Romeo and Juliet.

To be sure, such an interpretation appeals to modern people, who prefer emotional muddling to moral principle, ambiguity to clarity. In today's world, the ruling norm of validation in any moral choice is the level of discomfort endured in reaching it. In today's popular mind, every ethical decision is justified if it takes a sufficient toll on the emotions. Thus, Delilah's treatment of Samson, which earlier ages described as a shameless betrayal, might today be viewed as a regrettable but unavoidable personal dilemma ("a woman's right to choose"), morally justified if it entails adequate internal agonizing.

This raises the question of Delilah's motive, which is related to the matter of her nationality. After all, the Bible gives no clear indication that she was a Philistine or was prompted by a spirit of patriotism. Indeed, the evidence points in a different direction along both paths.

With respect to Delilah's nationality, we remark that Sorek Valley lay in the territory of Judah, not Dan. This detail does not support the case that she was a

Philistine. Moreover, when Delilah was approached by the plotting Philistines, the latter made no appeal to any patriotism on her part. Finally, we recall that an earlier Philistine woman had already broken faith with Samson (Judg. 14:15–19). Although we can hardly regard this Danite as the sharpest knife in the drawer, we would not expect him to be duped by a second female Philistine.

With respect to Delilah's motive, fear plays no part. It is instructive that the Philistines do not threaten her, as they threatened their earlier compatriot. On the contrary, they entice Delilah's greed with the promise of a reward. As far as the Bible is concerned, she is driven by no motive so noble as patriotism. She would simply like to have some cash. If the latter is available, there is not the faintest hesitation on the lady's part, much less a case of scruples. Indeed, there is nothing in the text to suggest that the Philistines have to do more than name their price, and Sweet Little D is primed for action.

If, as seems to be the case, Delilah belonged to the tribe of Judah, then Samson was betrayed to the Philistines by an insider. In this respect she resembles no one in the Bible more than Judas Iscariot, who also knew a thing or two about betrayal with kisses, provided the payment was sufficient.

In Delilah's case, the payment was ample. Each of the five Philistine lords promised her eleven hundred pieces of silver when the job was over, and Delilah, always good at math, made a prompt decision. If she entertained any doubts on the business, the Bible doesn't mention it. It would be laughable to do so.

CHAPTER 12

A Stubborn Mind

Now AND THEN I think that the biblical historians must have been men of modest expectations, in the sense that they tended to let people off easy. I have in mind the times when the biblical writers remark about this or that king, "he did what was right in the eyes of the Lord," and then go on to describe every manner of reprehensible behavior on the king's part. I fancy sometimes that "he did what was right in the eyes of the Lord" is really a code for "Well, after all, he could have been worse," or "At least he wasn't as bad as so-and-so," or "We can think of one or two sins he did not commit."

An egregious example of this, surely, is King Amaziah of Judah (796–767). Of him both 2 Kings (14:3) and 2 Chronicles (25:2) proclaim, "he did what was right in the eyes of the Lord," but then both sources proceed to paint a life in which one is hard-pressed to find a solitary thing that the eyes of the Lord could have found acceptable.

All right, I exaggerate. Amaziah did *one thing* that was right in the sight of the Lord—he did *not* retaliate on the families of his father's murderers (2 Kin. 14:6; 2 Chron. 25:4). *One thing*, then, he did right in the eyes of the Lord, and there you have it. The biblical writers, after exhaustive thought on the matter, were able to discover exactly one sin that Amaziah failed to commit. "He did what was right in the eyes of the Lord," it seems to me, is a pretty generous judgment on that fact. The rest of Amaziah's reign, not to put too fine a point on it, was a disaster.

Both biblical historians seem to sense the problem. Thus, immediately after announcing that Amaziah "did what was right in the eyes of the Lord," 2 Kings admits that he did not measure up to high moral standards set by David (who, if memory serves, was a murderer and adulterer). By way of explanation, the writer comments, as though to reassure the squeamish, that Amaziah "did in all things like Joash his father had done."

Now this is, to say the least, a dubious conces-
sion, inasmuch as Joash of Judah (who likewise, let
it be noted, "did what was right in the eyes of the
Lord"—2 Kin. 12:2) was an idolater and a murderer
(2 Chron. 24:18, 21, 25).

On the matter of Amaziah, the author of 2 Chronicles also hedges his bets. After declaring that the
king "did what was right in the eyes of the Lord,"
he promptly adds the disconcerting caveat, "but not
with a loyal heart." Oh, a heart problem? We will consider this later.

The Chronicler's treatment of Amaziah is longer
and more detailed. Whereas 2 Kings tells the story
of his invasion of Edom in just one verse (14:7), the
Chronicler needs nine verses (25:5–13). Only the
Chronicler, moreover, tells of the two prophets sent
to warn Amaziah (25:7–9, 15–16). Treating Amaziah's reign in greater detail, however, the Chronicler
inevitably makes him look worse.

We may begin with Amaziah's response to the
prophetic instruction against taking mercenaries
along for his invasion of Edom. When he complied
with that instruction, the mercenaries retaliated
against the king by sacking the villages and killing
the citizens of Judah (2 Kin. 25:13). Perhaps this was

the incident that turned Amaziah sour on prophecy, because the next time a prophet appears and starts to speak, Amaziah threatens him with death (25:16).

Then comes Amaziah's disastrous challenge to Joash, the king of Israel, where the difference between 2 Kings (14:8–14) and 2 Chronicles (25:17–24) is most noticeable. The difference lies in two details proper to the Chronicler.

First, the Chronicler introduces the story differently by mentioning that Amaziah "sought counsel" (*yiwa'ats*) before making his unwise challenge to Joash of Israel (2 Chron. 25:17). This verb, *ya'ats*, is a cognate of the noun *'etsah*, which was the last word in the preceding sentence, where the prophet tells the king, "I know that God has determined to destroy you, because you have done this and have not heeded *my counsel* (*'atsati*)" (25:16).

Thus, the counsel that Amaziah now seeks, counsel apparently sought from within his court, is contrasted with the counsel that he has just refused to accept from the prophet whom God sent to warn him. That is to say, Amaziah receives both bad and good counsel, but he walks "in the counsel of the ungodly" (*ba'atsath resha'im*—Ps. 1:1). Accordingly, Amaziah meets the biblical definition of a fool.

Only the Chronicler, anyway, notes these two counsels provided for Amaziah, and they form the structural frame for his assessment of the king.

Second, only the Chronicler explicitly tells of the Lord's intention to bring low the throne of Amaziah. This intention was also related directly to the king's refusal to hear prophetic counsel: "But Amaziah would not heed, for it came from God, that He might give them into the hand of their enemies, because they sought the gods of Edom" (2 Chron. 25:20). This interpretation of the events is related directly to the prophecy that followed that matter of the gods of Edom: "I know that God has determined to destroy you" (25:16).

Amaziah was a failure because he embraced the Edomite gods, the same gods that had already proved—as the prophet pointed out to him—so useless to the Edomites themselves (2 Chron. 25:14–15, 20). Across the brow of each of these gods was chiseled, as it were, the word *Loser,* and this may be taken as the final comment on Amaziah as well, because he exemplified Israel's most consistent sin—the foolish adoption of gods that had already been discredited. The Chronicler admitted that Amaziah's problem was his heart (25:2). The disloyalty of Amaziah's heart led, then, to the hardening of his ears. Such is the spiritual deafness associated with idolatry.

CHAPTER 13

Cowardice

A LL FOUR CANONICAL Gospels relate that Pilate, succumbing at last to the pressure of the mob, handed Jesus over to the unjust punishment of torture and death. Only Matthew (27:24–25), however, includes a final section of dialogue between Pilate and the people, just before Jesus was led away to torture. We will look at each side of this important dialogue—Pilate first, and then the people.

It begins: "When Pilate saw that he could not prevail at all, but rather that a tumult was rising, he took water and washed his hands before the multitude, saying, 'I am innocent of the blood of this man. You see to it.'"

In making this gesture, Pilate may have been counseled by some Jews. We suspect this, because the gesture—washing one's hands to convey innocence—was well known to the Jews (cf. Deut. 21:6–9; Ps. 25/26:6–10; Is. 1:15–16).

In fact, nonetheless, this was a duplicitous and hypocritical action in Pilate's case. Crucifixion was a Roman form of punishment, and Pilate represented Rome. The Jewish punishment for blasphemy, which was, after all, the charge brought against Jesus before the Sanhedrin, was stoning to death. We see this punishment exemplified in the death of Stephen, who also was condemned for blasphemy. It was the Romans, however, not the Jews, who crucified Jesus.

No matter, then, how much water touched Pilate's hands, the decision to execute Jesus was his to make, and he made it. Consequently, his protestation of innocence was hypocritical; he could have saved the life of an innocent man unjustly accused, exercising the justice that the Roman government had sent him to Judea to exercise. In handing Jesus over to death, then, Pilate violated man's law as well as God's.

One fancies that Pilate may have spent the rest of his days remarking, "Yes, it was the most difficult and painful decision I ever had to make." Such references to the difficulties of a moral choice are often invoked by way of excusing a bad moral decision. Such appeals are invariably self-serving, and in no case do they excuse the person from the moral evil of his choice. A sinful decision is still a sinful decision, no matter how difficult it was to make.

There is no narrative perspective, consequently, in which Pilate can be viewed as anything but a moral coward in condemning an innocent man to a terrible death in order to placate the demands of a mob. It was the whole boast of Roman authority that it imposed justice over mob rule.

In the year 381, when the bishops of the Church met at Constantinople to combat, once again, the heresies of the day, they determined to make a few (and, it happened, final) adjustments of the Creed promulgated at Nicaea in 325. Most of these adjustments consisted in additions to the Creed's third article, professing faith in the Holy Spirit and the Spirit's work in the Church and Holy Scripture.

They also added slight but significant refinements to the Creed's second article, on the being and activity of God's Son; these consisted entirely of small citations from Holy Scripture. One of these consisted of just three words taken from 1 Timothy 6:13—*epi Pontiou Pilatou*. So the final version of the final version of the Creed declares that Jesus was "crucified under Pontius Pilate."

Thus, in every recitation of the Nicene Creed since the end of the fourth century, explicit mention is made of the cowardice of that one man. To this very day, millions of men and women, and even little children, are reminded once again of the terrible sin of cowardice. The memory of Pilate, his weakness and betrayal of trust, is continually placed before the Christian mind, beginning with the rite of Baptism and repeated daily in the prayers of the Church.

CHAPTER 14

The Habit of Guile

WHETHER BY TEMPERAMENT or training, Laban of Haran was a shrewd man of business. Always able to sniff out profits and ever swift in their pursuit, he was constantly vigilant for new opportunities and additional sources of gain. *Interest* was his favorite noun, and *compound* his adjective of choice.

Thus, when Laban's sister Rebekah returned home from the well one day, accompanied by an elderly sojourner from afar, her brother made careful note of the man's apparel, the quality of his retinue, the number of his camels, and the enigmatic baggage by which the latter were burdened.

Laban observed, moreover, that Rebekah came back adorned with costly jewels she had not been wearing when she left home that day. Her brother then listened carefully while the visitor described himself as a servant on a mission to find a wife for the son of his wealthy master, who lived in the land of Canaan. Would Rebekah, the servant inquired, consent to become the wife of that wealthy man's son?

At least from Laban's viewpoint, the question was settled when "the servant brought out jewelry of silver, jewelry of gold, and clothing, and gave them to Rebekah. He also gave precious things to her brother and to her mother" (Gen. 24:53). Man of business that he was, Laban sensed the advantage of becoming the brother-in-law of a wealthy man, and he was relieved when his sister consented to the servant's proposal. Off she went to Canaan with the blessing of her brother.

A whole generation had passed when Laban received yet another visitor, this one the younger son of that sister who had departed. His name was Jacob, and Laban proceeded, by habit, to size him up. It was necessary, after all, that men of business should take the measure of other men and make estimates of their mettle. This activity was good for business.

Quickly sensing that Jacob was no match for him, Laban engaged the young man as an underpaid employee and then tricked him into marrying Leah, an inconvenient daughter who had proved too plain for other potential suitors in the neighborhood. From this experience Jacob learned the ways of Laban and began to form some estimates of his own. From that point on, the two men became competitors.

Laban, had he considered that this son of his sister shared his own blood and lineage, should have known better than to strain his association with Jacob. The latter, albeit still young, was to prove, in due course, more than a match for his uncle and father-in-law.

In fact, Jacob had already learned a thing or two about sizing men up and judging what they were made of. Shortly before arriving at Laban's house, he had correctly measured and tested his own twin brother, Esau, and thereby succeeded in taking possession of both the latter's birthright and his blessing.

In fact, wily Jacob had been very carefully observing that brother for quite some time, for a rivalry between the two had begun even before their birth. Heaven knows how it started. Apparently they were not identical twins (cf. Gen. 25:25; 27:11), and it is possible that Jacob was conceived first. Perhaps he felt a prior claim, as it were, on the womb of his

mother (to whom he would always remain the preferred son) and regarded his brother as an intruder.

However that may be, the two boys wrestled
together to determine which of them would be the
firstborn (Gen. 25:22). Esau won that contest, but even
as he issued forth into the air he felt the strong hand of
Jacob still gripping his heel in a trip hold (25:26).

It is significant that Jacob's very first encounter
with another human being was a struggle for suprem-
acy. The experience marked him for life. Even the
Almighty, when He determined to gain Jacob's attention, was obliged to turn the encounter into a wres-
tling match (Gen. 32:22–32).

This trait in Jacob's character also prepared him
for dealing with Laban. The latter's repeated attempts
to trick, defraud, and deceive him were met in every
instance by crafty countermeasures that left the older
man in a state of growing frustration. Gradually, and
with recourse to every ruse and ploy, Jacob managed
over the years to acquire much of Laban's property.
Finally, he gathered up all his goods and simply went
back to Canaan. Having left home years before with
only a staff in his hand, Jacob returned a man of wealth.

Both Laban and Esau are regarded without favor
in the later parts of the Bible. The Book of Wisdom,
describing the career of Jacob, dismisses both of

those men simply as "his enemies," who "oppressed him" and "lay in wait for him" (10:10–12). In the New Testament, Esau is called "a profane person" (Heb. 12:16), while Laban, that erstwhile man of business, is not named at all.

PART 3

Social Disorder

CHAPTER 15

Revising the Story

PERHAPS NO ONE else knew it, but the Ammonites nursed a grudge against Israel. They were persuaded that the Israelites were occupants of a large tract of Ammonite land, so they resolved by force of arms to take back what was theirs. Accordingly, "It came to pass after a time that the people of Ammon made war against Israel" (Judg. 11:4).

To meet this challenge, the Lord raised up Jephthah, who began by inquiring of these belligerents the reason for their hostility. The Ammonites rehearsed their historical grievance as best they could remember it: "Because Israel took away my land when they came up out of Egypt, from the Arnon as far as the Jabbok, and to the Jordan. Now, therefore, restore these lands peaceably" (Judg. 11:13).

Jephthah, who perceived a misunderstanding on the part of the Ammonites, went to some pains to spell out for them several points on which his memory of the matter differed significantly from theirs. First, he said, Israel had always been careful to respect the territorial integrity of its neighbors east of the Jordan (Judg. 11:14–18).

Second, the land under dispute had not belonged to the Ammonites anyway, but to another group called the Amorites. Moreover, the territory in question had been seized from the Amorites when the latter attacked Israel, not the other way around (Judg. 11:19–23).

In this reference to the ancient events narrated in Numbers 21:21–26, Jephthah also gently reminded the Ammonites that they themselves had formerly lived under Amorite rule, from which Israel had delivered them and restored them to their ancestral property (Judg. 11:24; cf. Num. 21:29–30). With this they should be satisfied. Indeed, for this they should be grateful.

Third, three hundred years had elapsed since all these things had happened (Judg. 11:26). Why had the matter never been brought up before?

We discern a pattern here. The Ammonites of the eleventh century BC were engaged in an exercise of historical revisionism, which consisted in treating old events with a new theory. Viewing history under the lens of a fresh interpretation, the Ammonites concluded that three centuries earlier they had suffered an injustice that now needed to be set right. That is to say, they wanted reparations for something they imagined to have happened three centuries earlier. Having lived in peace with Israel for three hundred years, they were now commencing a war for the purpose of correcting an alleged wrong from a time before even their grandparents were born.

It came to pass, of course, that the Ammonites failed in this endeavor. Their historical revisionism brought upon them only further suffering—indeed, "a very great slaughter" (Judg. 11:33).

History provides other examples, alas, of this Ammonite line of thought. For instance, some four centuries after Jephthah the Veientes went to war against Rome to recover territory that the Romans had earlier seized after defeating the Fidenates. For various reasons, the Veientes believed that the Fidenate land really belonged to themselves, so they had a right to take it from Rome by force. As Pliny (*History*

1.15) and Plutarch (*Romulus* 25) described the outcome of their efforts, however, the Veientes fared no better than the Ammonites.

The Ammonites, let it be said, seem ever to be with us. Their ideology may be described as attempting to remedy some ancient historical injustice—real or alleged—by taking action against the descendants of those accused of the injustice. They either want back their real estate, or they demand indemnities for injuries to their ancestors, or they require restitution for this or that offense of yesteryear. Such folk seem never to realize that this kind of thinking is radically fraudulent.

Now it is obvious that history does display wide patterns of real injustice, and no one denies that many people in the world still suffer from things that happened to their forebears a long time ago. It is a settled lesson of history, however, that efforts to go back and correct the past generally produce only more injustice. Most recorded attempts to rectify ancient historical wrongs serve chiefly to prove the thesis that "the wrath of man does not produce the righteousness of God" (James 1:20).

Moreover, few events in life are open to only one interpretation, even in their immediate context, and it is often the case that the passage of time renders their real moral character yet more ambiguous. Consequently, attempts to remedy the perceived wrongs of bygone times will almost certainly be regarded by others as merely unwarranted provocations. Such endeavors lead to further animosities, even wars.

In short, it is doubtful that the Ammonite ideology has ever really set right a single historical wrong, but it has most certainly given rise to many new ones.

CHAPTER 16

Domestic Conspiracy

THE ACCOUNT OF Ananias and Sapphira is arguably the most frightening story in the New Testament. We are scarcely surprised by St. Luke's comment that "great *fear* came upon all the Church and upon all who heard these things" (Acts 5:11).

In Luke's bright account of the grace of the Holy Spirit in the early Church, this terrible story serves as something like a sunspot. And, like a sunspot, it may escape our notice. We should study it, nonetheless, for much the same reason that astrophysicists study sunspots: Whether we study them or not, they are real and affect the atmosphere in which we live.

We may reflect on the account of Ananias and Sapphira along three lines of interest:

The first is their resistance to the Holy Spirit. This was, in fact, the explicit concern of St. Peter, when he asked Ananias, "Why has Satan filled your heart to lie to the Holy Spirit?" (Acts 5:3). Peter repeated this question to Sapphira, "How is it that you have agreed together to test the Spirit of the Lord?" (Acts 5:9).

In all the New Testament, this story may be our closest illustration of blasphemy against the Holy Spirit, that radical state of spiritual depravity which puts the offender outside the realm of mercy (cf. Mark 3:29).

The Old Testament does not mention this sin, perhaps because blasphemy against the Holy Spirit was not yet possible. The full measure of this sin is found only in the Church. I mean, this ultimate offense—the unequivocal repudiation of God's ultimate gift—is possible only when the gift has been received. Thus, the traditional sacramental discipline of the Church has always regarded the deliberate sins of Christians as more serious than the sins of pagans (Heb. 10:26–29).

Our second line of reflection is this: The sin of Ananias and Sapphira included a self-seeking and rapacious attitude toward material things. It is instructive to observe the verb Luke uses to speak of their sin. Peter questions Ananias: "Why has Satan filled your heart to lie to the Holy Spirit and misappropriate, for yourself, the price of the land?" (Acts 5:3).

Luke's Greek word for "misappropriate" is *nosphizein*, a verb rare in the Scriptures but used to refer to the sin of Achan in Joshua 7:1 (LXX). The latter scene describes how Achan violated the Lord's command to seize no spoils from the destruction of Jericho:

> But the children of Israel committed a great trespass and misappropriated (*enosphizanto*) the condemned things, for Achan the son of Carmi, the son of Zabdi, the son of Zerah, of the tribe of Judah, took the condemned things; so the anger of the Lord burned against the children of Israel.

The offense of Achan was the first sin of the Israelites after their entrance to the Promised Land. Employing the same verb, *nosphizein*, Luke likens this first sin of new Christians to that of ancient Achan. In each case there was the deliberate misappropriation of a blessing.

Our third line of reflection is this: The sin of Ananias and Sapphira was a conspiracy. Peter inquired of Sapphira, "How is it that you have conspired (*synephonethe*) to test the Spirit of the Lord?" (Acts 5:9).

Men are bad enough when they soil their own consciences. Conspiracy is an advanced state of sin. Sin is particularly malicious when it exploits the social institutions that are proper to human existence. Sin reaches its full potential when it takes on a social and institutional form.

Among human institutions, of course, the most basic is marriage. So, if we have likened Ananias and Sapphira to Achan, we should liken them also to Adam and Eve. Our first parents did not sin simply as individuals. Their offense was conspiratorial; they formed a pact of infidelity to the Lord.

Adam and Eve bonded together in the attempt to keep God's will out of their shared life. Right from the beginning, therefore, they polluted the institution of the family. Ananias and Sapphira repeated that conspiracy, nor were they the last couple to do so. It is far from uncommon to find husbands and wives conspiring to keep the Law of God out of their homes. It is part of the legacy of Adam and Eve.

From the story of Ananias and Sapphira we should take away at least these three lessons: the utter seriousness of the Holy Spirit, the danger of a rapacious attitude toward material things, and the great danger of using human institutions, especially the family, as the medium and setting of conspiracy against God's Law.

CHAPTER 17

Priestly Betrayal

EVER SINCE READING it many decades ago, I have wondered how anyone familiar with St. John Chrysostom's treatise on priestly ordination could still summon the nerve to place his bowed head under a bishop's hands. The message of that book has ever seemed to me: "Go ahead, fool, get yourself ordained; the devil is just waiting for you!"

Holy Scripture, too, speaks of the perils of the priesthood: Even as the rules for that institution were still being established, two brand-new priests, Nadab and Abihu, came abruptly to a bad end when they decided to get fancy with the censer. (I've seen this, actually.) Because a solemn warning on the subject of alcohol follows the story of their demise, I suspect the two new priests were intoxicated at the time (Lev. 10:1–9). Not good.

Another pair of unworthy priests were the two sons of Eli, Hophni and Phineas, who served the shrine at Shiloh. They, too, came to a sudden bad end (1 Sam. 4:11, 17), after ignoring their father's warning to mend their ways (2:23–25).

The offenses of Hophni and Phineas were not common moral failings, such as drunkenness; they were directly related, rather, to the ministry itself. That is to say, these two scoundrels used their priestly authority and position to take advantage of the very people for whom they were ordained (Heb. 5:1). Their sins were particularly heinous.

Holy Scripture mentions two abuses of Hophni and Phineas:

For one thing, they violated the trust of "the women who assembled at the door of the tabernacle" (1 Sam. 2:22). It was a sin of raw and crude exploitation: For the purpose of sexual gratification, they betrayed the confidence and exploited the vulnerabilities of those religious women, whom it was their responsibility to serve and care for. That is to say, their ministry in the Lord's house provided the very means and context of their infidelity.

The other offense of Hophni and Phineas involved

the act of sacrifice itself. Disdaining that part of the sacrificial victim assigned to the priest, these two scoundrels insisted on taking a "choice cut" from the offered meat prior to the sacrifice itself (1 Sam. 2:12–16). Thus, instead of serving the Lord's house, they made sure the Lord's house served them. This will always be the mark of an unworthy priest.

Following the lead of Venerable Bede's commentary on this story, we should regard those unworthy priests at Shiloh as foreshadowings of the later priests, chiefly Caiaphas, who condemned Jesus in the Sanhedrin and then accused Him before the judgment seat of Pontius Pilate. Indeed, it was at the home of Caiaphas that the whole plot was planned (Matt. 26:3–4). This supreme representative of the Jewish people used the very office of his ministry—the worship of God—to murder God's Son. Even Pilate read the motive as envy (27:18; cf. 21:38).

Thus, Caiaphas remains for all time the egregious example of a genuinely rotten priest.

At the same time, the Gospel writers were aware of the irony involved in that singular betrayal of the priestly office: By condemning Jesus to death (Matt. 26:63–66), this unworthy priest unwittingly provided the means of God's perfect worship, the unique and supreme sacrifice to take away the sins of the world.

Given even the minimum standards for the ministry—"blameless, the husband of one wife, temperate, sober-minded, of good behavior, hospitable, able to teach; not given to wine, not violent but gentle, not quarrelsome, not covetous" (1 Tim. 3:2–3)—it is not surprising that we find the occasional minister who doesn't measure up.

I fear the worst examples, however, are not those weak individuals who carry on a double life—priests with a gambling problem, for example, or drunken priests, even priests who violate their marriage vows. Although the canons of the Church properly bar such men from priestly ministry, their offenses are essentially manifestations of weakness, not malice.

Far worse, certainly, are those offenses associated with the very exercise of the priesthood, sins directly concerned with the setting and context of the ministry, such as the quest for power and absolute control. I have in mind the violation of trust in matters of conscience, the cultivation of malice in place of mercy, the disposition to answer criticism with revenge, and the abuse of authority to tyrannize the hearts and minds of the Lord's flock. Such offenses come closer to the sins of Eli's sons and, more ominously, the unspeakable crime of Caiaphas.

CHAPTER 18

Nasty Religious People

I T WOULD BE a comfort to think that all those who go up to the house of the Lord are led there by the Holy Spirit. It would also be an illusion. Even if experience did not testify that people sometimes attend worship with the most deplorable attitudes and for the worst possible reasons, Holy Scripture itself would caution us to realism on the point.

An early example, I suppose, is Peninnah, Elkanah's "other wife," who used the annual pilgrimage to Shiloh as an opportunity to render life miserable for barren Hannah. The latter she tormented severely, says the Sacred Text, to make her miserable. The provocation was not unintentional, we are assured, nor did it happen only once: "So it was, year by year, when she went up to the house of the Lord, that she provoked her; therefore she wept and did not eat" (1 Sam. 1:6–7). It is easy to picture Peninnah looking forward to that annual pilgrimage with the family; it was perhaps her favorite time of the year, providing her the forum for feeling superior and spreading discouragement.

Now, as it happened, the God who brings good out of evil caused everything to work out well for Hannah, and the story soon turns into an account of grace and divine visitation. Still, there was a serious pastoral problem at Shiloh, and I suspect more than one worshipper at the time wished the priest Eli, pointing to Peninnah, would suggest to Elkanah, "When your family comes next year, brother, why not leave Miss Picklepuss at home?" I do believe that Eli's failure to intervene was among his several shortcomings.

Oh that Peninnah was history's last recorded example of a surly, mean-spirited individual using the time of divine worship as the occasion to make someone else feel wretched and forlorn!

Not so, however. Another is the gospel story of the ruler of the synagogue, a singularly unattractive, grumpy person who objected to Jesus' healing of a crippled woman on the Sabbath. In the midst of the spontaneous praise of God that ensued upon that gracious deed, this particular bellyacher felt it his duty to sound a warning to the congregation about liturgical proprieties: "There are six days on which men ought to work," he declared, "therefore come and be healed on them, and not on the Sabbath day" (Luke 13:14). Quick to pass judgment on others and blinded by his own vicious, miserly spirit, this religious leader was unable to recognize the divine presence and the outpouring of grace.

Devoid of mercy, we notice, he was also without courage. Consequently, instead of confronting Jesus directly, this coward had recourse to what had always worked for him in the past—he harangued the congregation about the woman herself!

It is often declared—and more often, perhaps, than is true—that churches are full of hypocrites. Here was one occasion, however, when the Lord really did use that very noun to describe someone in the place of worship. Unlike Eli, who failed to give a proper pastoral admonition to Elkanah, Jesus turned his not-amused attention to this so-called ruler of the synagogue: "Hypocrite! Does not each one of you on the Sabbath loose his ox or donkey from the stall, and lead it away to water it?" (Luke 13:15).

The Lord's indignation in this setting, which was scarcely untypical of him (cf. Mark 3:5), suggests that a pastor's patience in these circumstances should not be unlimited. Peninnah and the ruler of the synagogue behaved like wolves, not like sheep. They needed to be treated like wolves. The Lord gives here an example of the proper pastoral response to situations in which an individual apparently comes to church for the purpose of making other people in church miserable. Such folk need either to repent or stay home.

I began these comments by mentioning that not all church attendance seems to be prompted by the Holy Spirit, an impression that opens the possibility of other spirits at work. One hates to consider this possibility, but there is evidence that some individuals are led to congregations for the demonic purpose of doing harm. Early in Christian history, both the *Didache* and *The Travels of Egeria* mention the testing needed to settle that question. When a pastor admits someone into the congregation, we presume he is able to distinguish a sheep from a wolf. Indeed, we very much depend on it.

CHAPTER 19

Industrial Waste

EVERYBODY, I SUPPOSE, has his own favorite among the ten plagues inflicted on Egypt. Mine is number six.

On the outside chance, however, that its finer details may have slipped the reader's mind, let us quickly rehearse the account. The Lord said to Moses and Aaron:

> Take for yourselves handfuls of ashes from a kiln, and let Moses scatter them toward heaven in the sight of Pharaoh. And it will become fine dust in all the land of Egypt, and it will cause boils that break out in sores on man and beast throughout all the land of Egypt. (Ex. 9:8–8)

Several features of this plague seem to stand out. It involves, for instance, a sort of ritual. Whereas the previous plagues appeared without much ceremony—at most, the extension of Aaron's rod—in this case Moses must go and gather some ashes that he flings heavenward. There is a more obvious cause and effect here. These ashes become (*wəhaya*) the afflicting dust.

The ashes, moreover, are taken from a kiln (*kibshan*), an industrial furnace used either to smelt metallic ore or to bake bricks. The important thing to consider is that this kibshan represented the economic and cultural life of Egypt.

This detail is significant. When the Book of Exodus earlier spoke of the hardships the Egyptians imposed on the Israelites, it spoke in particular of the baking of bricks for the Pharaoh's building projects (1:14; 5:7–19). The Egyptian construction technology resembled, in this respect, that of ancient Babel (Gen. 11:3). Indeed, there was an even deeper, more spiritual affinity in the two cases; the ambitions of Babel and Egypt displayed the same political idolatry, the identical rebellion against the true God.

Thus, when Moses throws the ashes from this kiln "heavenward," the action symbolized Egypt's pride and rebellion against God. The text says that Moses did this "at the eyes of Pharaoh." That is to say, the ashes are thrown toward heaven, but they are also thrown at Pharaoh's eyes; flung in the latter direction they symbolize the spiritual blindness the king displays through the entire course of the plagues.

A modern reader of Exodus can hardly fail to suspect in this story an ecological dimension; the sixth plague involved a measure of air pollution when Moses removes the ashes from the furnace and casts them into the atmosphere. That is to say, the severe skin rash on the flesh of the Egyptians came from industrial waste, specifically air pollution. The story sounds terribly modern.

I don't believe such a reading is far-fetched, however, inasmuch as part of the message in the early chapters of Exodus is the oppressive nature of Egypt's economic and technical culture. Already in Genesis, indeed, the same idolatrous impulse had been present in the brick-and-bitumen works of ancient Babel, and the same theme we find later in the social concerns of the prophets. William Blake was on solid biblical ground when he spoke of "the dark satanic mills" to describe the Industrial Revolution (in his poem "And did those feet in ancient time").

The wound inflicted by the dust of this plague is called a *shechin*, apparently an inflammation (from the root *shachan,* meaning "to be hot"). The Septu-agint version translates this term as *elkos,* meaning "an abscess or ulceration." This is exactly the term that appears in the Bible's final set of plagues, those in the Book of Revelation. Of the first of those plagues we read, "So the first [angel] went and poured out his bowl upon the earth, and a foul and loathsome abscess (elkos) came upon the men who had the mark of the Beast and those who worshiped his image" (Rev. 16:2).

Once again, this plague is a punishment for the sin of idolatry; it afflicts "the men who had the mark of the Beast and those who worshiped his image."

When the Beast and his mark were first mentioned three chapters earlier, the context was a form of idol-atry expressed in social and economic oppression. Of this Beast we are told, "He causes all, both small and great, rich and poor, free and slave, to receive a mark on their right hand or on their brow, and that no one may buy or sell except one who has the mark or the name of the beast, or the number of his name" (Rev. 13:15).

The mark of the Beast, inscribed on the forehead or the right hand of the idolaters, is a parody of the seal that marks the brow of those who worship the Lamb (Rev. 7). This very seal was foreshadowed in the paschal blood which, on Passover night, marked the doorframes of the Israelites in Egypt. In the end-time, then, humanity is divided by these two marks.

Inasmuch as the service of a false god invariably fosters some form of servile domination, idolatry is never a victimless crime. Pharaoh, because his heart is hard, will always be an oppressor.

CHAPTER 20

Risking the Millstone

REAL PAGANS, IF they are also good and sane pagans, are obliged to agree on certain rules among themselves, some established set of common expectations in order to render social existence even possible. They must set up minimum social standards of behavior, with a view to discouraging murder, adultery, fraud, and other conduct harmful to one another or the common good.

In pursuit of this purpose, such pagans promulgate laws, establish forums of adjudication, and provide for sanctions against offenders. They exert this effort simply in order to survive. This cooperative effort is what philosophers call the social contract, which strives to preserve at least a manageable level of public decency and order, sufficient to make civic life possible, perhaps even enjoyable.

The goals of a decent, stable society are modest. Its standards are not necessarily demanding. It has in mind to form citizens, not saints. It does not command holiness. It does not require fast days and the maintenance of vigils. It imposes on no one the obligation to strive for sanctity, and—except during wartime and national disasters—it does not normally exact strenuous asceticism or heroic virtue of its citizens.

On the other hand, a society of this sort should hardly feel threatened when some of its own members, not entirely satisfied with the modest goals of civic life, desire to strive for something higher. Ordinarily a good, sane pagan society should have no objection to a few saints and ascetics in its midst, as long as these saints and ascetics are also solid citizens.

Early Christian apologists made this point over and over, tirelessly explaining to the pagans of their own day that the higher calling of the Christian faith posed no threat to the stability and well-being of ordinary society. Justin, Tertullian, and their friends assured their fellow citizens that Christians, precisely because they held themselves to a more demanding spiritual criterion, could always be counted on to maintain the minimum expectations of the social order. They affirmed this with great confidence.

To the chagrin of reasonable pagans, however, it sometimes happens that those professing adherence to the higher norms of religious faith nonetheless fall below—even far below—the elementary, minimum level of goodness expected in a decent society.

For example, the Books of Maccabees, which describe at length the severe pagan persecution of the Jews during the second century before Christ, tell also of the scandals caused in the pagan world by very bad but highly placed Jews. Among the worst of such scandals was the one created by a character named Menelaus, who simply outbid the previous high priest, Jason, who also had obtained that office by bribery. Indeed, by his cunning use of riches stolen from the temple treasury, Menelaus became for a while a major player in the geopolitics of the Middle East.

The treachery of Menelaus was shocking even to the pagans of his time. When he arranged for the murder of Onias, an earlier high priest, the bloody deed touched the moral sensitivity of the whole region, even of that cruel persecutor of the Jews, Antiochus IV Epiphanes (2 Macc. 4:35–38). Later, when a delegation of Jews complained of Menelaus to the king, this same high priest arranged to have *them* murdered as well, an act that horrified even the Phoe-nicians, a people not especially sensitive on moral questions (4:44–49).

Alas, this seems rather often to be the case. How are pagans to take seriously those who profess to be better than the world, when in fact they live by norms conspicuously lower than the world? How is it possible for a Christian church to hold its bishops, for instance, to lower ethical expectations in matters of business than the chairman of a secular corporation? Why are such scandals permitted, year after year? Or again, why should a priest not be unfrocked for offenses that would promptly send a school counselor to prison? How can we expect pagans to take any Christian church seriously if it does not call its own stewards to account?

Alas, it is a demonstrable fact that the people of God, when they fall, often enough do not fall to the level of good paganism, but much lower. They sink down so far that even the law-abiding pagan is bewildered. And this bewilderment constitutes scandal in that word's strict sense, because it testifies that the people of God are truly bad people. It convinces the unbeliever that Christians are hypocrites who do not truly believe what they declare.

Clearly this reflection bears on the relationship between church discipline and the ministry of evangelism. If the gospel is to be taken seriously by the contemporary pagan culture that surrounds us, it is imperative that the churches speak with the voice of authority to the moral lives of their members—especially holding its own leadership to account—because nothing eviscerates evangelism more effectively than scandal.

PART 4

Sin and Politics

CHAPTER 21

The Cultivation of Arrogance

ACCORDING TO THE custom of counting both the first and last years of his time on the throne (793–742), Uzziah was Judah's longest reigning monarch, fifty-two years (2 Chron. 26:3). During those final years, however, he shared the throne with his son, Jotham (26:21). In spite of this lengthy reign, Uzziah is treated in 2 Kings (15:1–7) in a mere seven verses. Clearly the author did not think much of him.

The Chronicler, whose more detailed account gives a better idea of Uzziah's importance, distinguishes this king in six respects.

First, he mentions the tutelage provided for Uzziah by the priest Zechariah (2 Chron. 26:5), whom he sees as a parallel to the ancient Jehoiada, the spiritual father of King Joash (24:2). Each king, then, receives early guidance from a priest.

Second, this feature is part of an obvious and more extensive correspondence, in the Chronicler's mind, between Joash and Uzziah. Both men began well, a fact that prompted the Bible to say that each man "did what was right in the eyes of the Lord" (2 Chron. 24:2; 26:4). In both of them the moral problem was one of growing arrogance that became manifest only later in their lives.

In each case, too, the king's fall is in some way connected to the Temple. In the instance of Joash, who at the beginning of his career "set his heart on repairing the house of the Lord" (2 Chron. 24:4), the royal defection came in the form of admitting idols into the Temple (24:17–18) and then killing the priest who reprimanded him for it (24:19–22).

In the case of Uzziah, the offense is also directed to the Temple, where the king attempted to usurp the proper role of the priests (2 Chron. 26:16). In this instance as well he is reprimanded by the priest (26:17–18) and, like Joash before him (24:21–22), Uzziah becomes very angry (26:19). This time, however, the Lord intervenes, so the king is unable to act on his wrath.

Third, only the Chronicler spells out all the details of Uzziah's military interests and exploits (2 Chron.

26:6–9, 11–15). Archaeology has uncovered several of the military installations mentioned in these verses, and from a worldly perspective Uzziah was certainly among Judah's greatest kings. For this reason it is significant that neither biblical historian has all that much to say about him.

Fourth, only the Chronicler speaks of Uzziah's pronounced enthusiasm for agriculture and animal husbandry: "He dug many wells, for he had much livestock, both in the lowlands and in the plains; he also had farmers and vinedressers in the mountains and in Carmel, for he loved the soil" (2 Chron. 26:10). This note strengthens our assessment of the prosperous reign of Uzziah.

Fifth, only the Chronicler gives the reason for Uzziah's leprosy, which affliction is recorded in 2 Kings (2 Chron. 26:21). The Chronicler regards the leprosy as a punishment for the king's proud usurpation of the priestly ministry (26:16–21), and his inclusion of this story expresses his sustained interest in the ministry and privileges of the authentic priesthood.

In respect to this offense and punishment, Uzziah's rejection by God corresponds to two earlier instances in biblical history. First, his leprosy immediately puts the reader in mind of Miriam, who was also made a leper for her revolt against the leadership of Moses (Num. 12:1–10). Second, the king's illegitimate assumption of priestly rites is a repetition of the sin of Saul, whom the Lord rejected for the same reason (1 Sam. 13:8–14).

Sixth, the Chronicler alone relates King Uzziah to the rise of literary prophecy in the eighth century: "Now the rest of the acts of Uzziah, from first to last, the prophet Isaiah the son of Amoz wrote" (2 Chron. 26:22). Because Isaiah himself, in the sixth chapter of his book, describes a mystical vision in the Temple "in the year that King Uzziah died," it is possible that this verse in Chronicles refers to the first five chapters of Isaiah. Both Amos and Hosea also prophesied during the time of Uzziah, albeit in the Northern Kingdom (Amos 1:1; Hos. 1:1).

The Bible's final word on Uzziah is not encouraging, for he is accused of arrogance and anger (2 Chron. 26:16–19). The prophet Isaiah, who probably was not even born when Uzziah came to the throne, seems to intend a contrast between Judah's longest reigning king and the Lord, the true king of His people: "In the year that King Uzziah died, I saw the Lord sitting on a throne, high and lifted up" (Is. 6:1). That is to say, Uzziah is at last in his grave, but the Lord is still on the Throne.

CHAPTER 22

The Gospel and the Sword

A<small>LTHOUGH THE APOSTLE</small> Peter enthusias-
tically confessed the identity of Jesus, he was
much slower in accepting the message of the Cross.
In fact, when Jesus first spoke of His coming Passion,
Peter's immediate response was, "Far be it from you,
Lord; this shall not happen to you!" (Matt. 16:22).

So Jesus, having declared Peter "blessed" for his
profession of faith, was obliged—within the span
of just a few verses—to tell him, "Get behind me,
Satan! You are an offense to me, for you are not
mindful of the things of God, but the things of men"
(Matt. 16:16–23).

How did Peter accept this reproof? The Gospels
do not inform us, in so many words, but a later story

indicates that the apostle did not take it very well. At least, the message seems not to have sunk in. Let me elaborate.

Everyone knows that Peter, during Jesus' trial before the Sanhedrin, denied even knowing him. According to the Gospel records, Peter made this denial three times. I want to suggest, however, that Peter, earlier that same night, had already denied what Jesus stood for. Before explicitly denying Jesus, Peter had already repudiated the message of the Cross.

The episode I have in mind was described by Matthew: "And suddenly, one of those who were with Jesus stretched out his hand and drew his sword, struck the servant of the high priest, and cut off his ear" (Matt. 26:51). This incident at the time of Jesus' arrest was strong evidence that Peter still was "not mindful of the things of God, but the things of men."

Moreover, the story of the severed ear conveys an ironic symbolism: Bearing in mind that "faith *comes* by hearing" (Rom. 10:17), we are perhaps justified in understanding this man's loss of an ear as a sort of impediment to faith. Peter amputated the very organ through which a human being normally has access to the gospel. That is to say, Peter's assumption of the sword that night, which effectively repudiated the message of the Cross, had the effect of impeding faith.

Peter's task, as an apostle, was to bring people to faith, but it was quite impossible for him to do that if he behaved in a way that impeded access to Christ. Thus, when he swung that sword at the high priest's servant, Peter effectively renounced the ministry for which Christ had chosen him.

Comparing Peter's action in this scene with his later denial of Jesus in the high priest's courtyard, I am disposed to believe the former sin worse than the latter. After all, when Peter denied Jesus to the servant maid and others, he was acting in weakness; he was afraid. When, however, he swung that sword at the head of the high priest's servant, he was acting in arrogance, pride, coercion, and recourse to worldly power.

A lesson to be drawn from this story is clear enough, but it is instructive how slow the Church has been to learn it.

Peter represents the Church in an official and authorized capacity. No matter how Christians variously interpret Jesus' mandate to him—"I will give you the keys of the kingdom of heaven" (Matt. 16:19)—they have long recognized in Peter's ministry an institutional aspect. He represents the Christian body in an official capacity. It is Peter's name at the top of the Church's stationery, so to speak.

As believers are accustomed to regard the ministry of Paul as prophetic, and that of John as contemplative, so they are disposed to see in Peter a certified spokesman for the official Church. This is hardly surprising, since in the Gospels Peter habitually functions that way.

Consequently, Peter's assumption of the sword— just hours after his "ordination" at the Last Supper— is extremely problematic. It raises the question: Is the official Church no different from a worldly institution? Are we to expect the authorized spokesmen for the gospel to behave like other men who wield power? It is true that few official churchmen—Pope Julius II comes to mind—have actually taken up a literal sword to assert their place among the powerful of the earth. But it is not unknown for those who enjoy high authority in the Church to lay hold of equivalent instruments. Peter was hardly the last Church official to impose his coercive will by intimidation. When this happens, however, someone's ear is cut off, and the gospel is not heard.

CHAPTER 23

The Vengeful Soul

O UR EARLIEST INTERPRETATION of the Book of Esther is the pre-Christian version found in the Septuagint. This version contains not only a Greek translation of the original book but also extensive textual interpolations that provide, in fact, a theological exposition of the story.

One of these interpolations is the second decree of King Ahasuerus (called Artaxerxes in this Greek version), the decree sought by Mordecai in order to neutralize the king's earlier decree authorizing the annihilation of the Jews (Esth. 8:9–13). Unlike the original Hebrew account, the Greek version provides a text of the decree itself (which in due course became 16:1–24 in St. Jerome's unhappy adjustment of the Latin text of Esther in the Vulgate).

An important object sought in this second decree, let me suggest, is to provide a philosophical reflection on the problem of political power. King Ahasuerus, in order to condemn the recent activity of the wicked Haman, commences on a more general note.

The king mentions the arrogance and cruelty sometimes engendered in the hearts of unworthy men who find themselves in positions of political power. This occurs, says the king, because such men forget "the justice of God, who sees all things and hates evil" (Esth. 8.12δ). Politics is hazardous, because it places men in control of great power, and great power, of its own nature, has a disposition to overwhelm and seize control of the very men who exercise it.

This danger especially obtains in the case of dishonorable individuals, men of diminished character. Is there anything more perilous than a morally weak man's possession of power? If the study of history had not already versed us in this lesson, the king concludes, the recent case of Haman certainly renders the matter clear.

Some readers of the Bible may recall, in this respect, Lord Acton's dictum that "power tends to corrupt" (Letter to Archbishop Mandell Creighton,

Apr. 5, 1887). It is important to note, I think, that Acton did not say, "power corrupts." Indeed, if that were the case, we could never have sound and wise government at all. What Acton said, rather, is that "power *tends* to corrupt." He spoke only of a tendency, a disposition, an abiding source of temptation. Like all temptations, it must be resisted. The problem is that individuals of diminished character, men unaccustomed to resisting temptation generally, are those most likely to succumb to this one in particular.

The king's decree indicates the danger of placing morally weak men in positions of power. (He conveniently doesn't mention that he himself gave Haman that power!) Political authority is prudently committed to the strong, the true men of character, especially those accustomed to the steady restraint of self-control. Surely, the first and only safe control is self-control. A man unable to govern himself cannot wisely be entrusted with the governance of anyone else (a family, for instance).

This was the case of Haman, who was no match for the tendency of power to corrupt, and in Haman's case—yet to abide with Acton—absolute power corrupted absolutely.

When the Book of Esther began, Haman was in no danger. If he did not engage in the reprehensible behavior recorded in this book, there is every reason to believe that he would live successfully to a ripe old age. He has only himself to blame for what befalls him. Conspiring to exact a ruthless, inordinate revenge for a slight offense magnified by his own grieved imagination, Haman does not realize that he plots his own ruin. Everything that happens to him he brings upon himself. Haman is no tragic figure. He is not the victim of a cruel fate. He is the casualty of his choices, the final recipient of his own hatred and cruelty.

There is immense irony in the story of Haman of course, but he himself is scarcely an ironical figure. Indeed, he is the very straightforward example of a certain biblical type—namely, the Fool. Haman begins his downfall with unbridled ambition, goes on to petty resentment, and at last lets a wild rancor eat away his heart. His is a steady decline into folly and cruelty.

Toward the end, there is no gauging the magnitude of the thing. He prepares for Mordecai a gallows eighty-five feet tall (Esth. 5:14), an excess embodying his total lack of reasoned measure, and on that gallows he is executed, devoured by forces larger than himself. Haman's outward demise only certifies a deeper death within.

CHAPTER 24

The Pride of Life

WHEN THE AUTHOR of Kings starts to tell
of Adonijah's attempt to seize the Davidic
throne (1 Kin. 1:5–10), he portrays both the man
and the event in ways that recall the earlier revolt
of Absalom.

Both brothers are described as handsome (1 Kin.
1:6; 2 Sam. 14:25), and each, acting in secrecy (1 Kin.
1:10; 2 Sam. 15:9–11), provides for himself not only
the identical showy retinue (1 Kin. 1:5; 2 Sam. 15:1)
but also the support of political figures at court (1
Kin. 1:7–8; 2 Sam. 15:31).

In addition, the author later reveals that Adonijah
entertains an amorous interest in Abishag, the new-
est of David's wives (1 Kin. 2:13–22); this detail, too,

puts the reader in mind of Absalom's public seizure of David's harem (2 Sam. 16:20–22).

These points of similarity form an analogy signif-icant to the author's intent, inasmuch as the reader already knows what became of Absalom. The literary scholar Meir Sternberg puts his finger on the matter. The author, he says, "directs the reader to apply the lessons of the past to the imminent conflict: to look forward to the new pretender's downfall while he appears at the zenith of his fortunes" (*The Poetics of Biblical Narrative*, 268).

The action happens at Ein-Rogel, a place named for the spring in the southern outskirts of Jerusalem, on the boundary line between the tribes of Judah and Benjamin (cf. Josh. 15:7; 18:16). Near Ein-Rogel lie the village of Siloam and the large flat-stone forma-tion called Zoheleth (Serpent's Stone), where Adon-ijah exploits his aged father's weakness by plotting to advance his own ambition. Taking advantage of a clan festival, Adonijah gathers the forces he needs to accomplish the coup, even though David is still alive and has not publicly declared his appointed heir.

Adonijah's claim to the throne is legally plausi-ble; his older brothers, Amnon and Absalom, are both dead, and perhaps Chileab (2 Sam. 3:3), so

Adonijah can promote his case on the premise of primogeniture.

The matter is murky, nonetheless, and the prince's failure to invite Solomon to the gathering at Ein-Rogel suggests that Adonijah knows, or at least, seriously suspects that David had Solomon in mind as his successor.

What Adonijah *does*, however, is not only murky; it is also dangerous. Even though he has the support of the rest of his siblings, at least some of the army (led by Joab), the priest Abiathar, and other officials of the court, the success of this coup depends on a certain measure of secrecy. The royal garden at Ein-Rogel (according to Josephus, *Antiquities of the Jews*, 7.14.4) is sufficiently secluded to avoid too much notice until the deed is actually done.

If we compare the names on Adonijah's guest list with the parallel list of those not invited, the most notable name among the latter is the Prophet Nathan. The author thus makes it plain that Adonijah has no prophetic support for his plan.

In this detail, we touch an emphasis fundamental to the intent of the book: God's continued guidance of His people through the oracles of the prophets. In the history of both the Southern and

Northern Kingdoms, we will find this to be a sustained motif. In fact, the author devotes to two of the prophets, Elijah and Elisha, more space than anyone except Solomon.

And when, near the end of the book, he describes the kingdom's downfall, he is careful to mention that it took place "according to the word of the Lord which He had spoken by His servants the prophets" (2 Kin. 24:2).

In his neglect of prophetic revelation, Adonijah demonstrates an insouciance to God's will and guidance. This is the first of many examples of royal arrogance throughout the period covered in Kings.

The young prince's resolve to "exalt himself," moreover, illustrates the biblical principle that whoever exalts himself will be humbled. Indeed, in attempting to usurp what does not yet belong to him, Adonijah is something of an Adam-figure; the Fall of humanity's original father, we remember, was likewise an attempt to seize an honor that was not yet his.

There is also a parallel between Adonijah and Saul, both of whom acted *preemptively*, not waiting for God's appointed time (cf. 1 Sam. 13:7–14). Both men are contrasted with David, who—albeit already anointed—never sought to seize the throne while Saul yet lived.

Expanding our comparisons to the full biblical canon, we may think of a certain New Testament character, as well, of whom St. John said, "I wrote to the church, but Diotrephes, who loves to have the preeminence among them, does not receive us" (3 John 9).

CHAPTER 25

Hostile Power

W HEN THE OBSCURE kingdom of Lydia came to geopolitical notoriety in the seventh century before Christ, the man responsible for its rise was a ruthless, warring king named Gugu (c. 680–c. 648).

Gugu was, at least, the name by which the Assyrians called him. Indeed, the earliest extant texts mentioning this Lydian king are found in the clay archives of the Assyrian emperor Ashurbanipal (668–633), who was for a while Gugu's suzerain lord. Now it is surely significant of Gugu's political and military importance that a fragment of earthen tablet in distant Mesopotamia contains our earliest inscription of his name.

In Mesopotamian memory, in fact, the name of Gugu lingered on in popular and literary memory.

Ezekiel, writing his prophecies in that same area during the next century (chapters 38—39), remembered the famous Lydian king as Gug or Gog (the two forms being identical in unmarked Hebrew).

Because of Lydia's inclusion in the greater world of the Greeks, it is no wonder that this latter people also spoke of Gugu (whose name they Hellenized to Gyges, our own *y* and the *u* being identical in Greek). In extant sources, the first Greek to mention Gugu was his contemporary, the poet Archilochus, who referred especially to the Lydian's great wealth. Aristotle quotes a line of Archilochus, "*Ou moi ta Gugeo tou polychrysou melei, oud' heile po me zelos*" (I am not bothered by the wealth of Gugu, nor did I ever envy him) (*Rhetoric,* 1418.42b).

Gugu's fame, as time went on, refused to fade. A full two centuries after his death, the Greek historian Herodotus (c. 482–c. 425) recorded memorable tales about him. In a rather involved story, for instance, he described how the wife of Gugu's predecessor persuaded him to kill her husband and seize the throne (*Histories,* 1.8–12). Other versions of this narrative (for example, Plato's *Republic,* 2.3 359C–360B) differ in the details, but most agree that Gugu murdered his predecessor and married the widow.

Gugu's violent seizure of the Lydian throne would have led to a civil war, says Herodotus (*Histories,* 1.13), except that the Delphic oracle confirmed the usurper in his new position. In gratitude for this, Gugu devoted many gifts to the Delphic shrine (*Histories,* 1.14).

No sooner had Gugu taken the throne than he began to wage war on all his neighbors. In fact, says Herodotus, "he accomplished nothing else of note (*ouden gar mega*) in his reign of thirty-eight years" (*Histories,* 1.15).

Gugu's great military success was partly purchased by his alliance with the Assyrians, nor could it long outlive that alliance. When, sometime about 648, Gugu sent forces to Egypt to help Pharaoh Psamtik I (664–610) in his rebellion against Ashurbanipal, the latter abandoned him to his local enemies in and around Lydia. That was the end of Gugu.

As we have seen, however, something about Gugu declined to die. In popular imagination he remained for centuries the very type of the barbarian warrior.

Thus, when the prophet Ezekiel, exiled in Mesopotamia a hundred years later, wanted to describe for his own contemporaries the coming judgment of God in the tumultuous events of history, all he had to do was invoke the name of Gugu, or Gog, to describe a menacing barbarian army.

This coming Gog, the prophet declares, holds sway in the land of Magog, a name meaning "(derived) from Gog" (Hebrew *min-Gog*). He is "the head (*rosh*) of Meshech and Tubal" (Ezek. 38:2), the two sons of Japheth and the fathers of most of the world's nations (Gen. 16:2; 1 Chron. 1:5; cf. Ezek. 27:13; 32:26; 39:1). This barbarian Gog represents, therefore, the hostile world arrayed for the invasion of God's people.

Six hundred years after Ezekiel, St. John wrote another prophetic book, which he sent to—among other places—Sardis (Rev. 3:1), the ancient capital of Lydia, the very place where Gugu had seized the throne and married the queen.

In this book, too, John prophesied that old Gog, along with Magog, was coming back after a thousand years to visit devastation on the earth: "Satan will be released from his prison and will go out to deceive the nations which are in the four corners of the earth, Gog and Magog, to gather them together to battle, whose number is as the sand of the sea" (Rev. 20:7–8).

Whereas the pagan world recalled Gugu mainly as the type of a ruthless warrior, the Bible sees him more as an enemy of God and an abiding threat to God's people. In either case, Gugu remains in this world, a very real problem. He has assumed many forms over the centuries.

CHAPTER 26

The Taste of Blood

O NE OF THE cruelest, most distressing stories in the Bible records how Athaliah, the *gebirah* or queen mother of the slain King Ahaziah, seized the throne of Judah in 841 BC and promptly ordered the murder of her own grandchildren in order to guarantee her hold on that throne (2 Kin. 11; 2 Chron. 22). Holy Scripture simply records the event without accounting for Athaliah's motive in this singular atrocity.

Although such savagery from a daughter of Jezebel might not be surprising, Athaliah's action was puzzling from a political perspective, nonetheless, and this in two respects. First, as the story's final outcome would prove, her dreadful deed rendered Athaliah extremely unpopular in the realm, and her possession of the crown, therefore, more precarious.

Second, had she preserved the lives of her grand-children, instead of killing them, Athaliah's real power in the kingdom would likely have been enhanced in due course, not lessened. As the gebirah, she might have remained the de facto ruler of Judah unto ripe old age. Just what, then, did the lady have in mind in this slaughter of her own grandchildren?

The historian Josephus, the first to speculate on this question, ascribed Athaliah's action to an inherited hatred of the Davidic house. It was her wish, said he, "that none of the house of David should be left alive, but that the entire family should be exterminated, that no king might arise from it later" (*Antiquities of the Jews*, 9.7.1).

The playwright Racine developed this very plausible explanation in his *Athalie*, where the evil queen exclaims, "David I abhor, and the sons of this king, though born of my blood, are strangers to me" (2.7.729–730).

Following Racine, this interpretation was taken up in Felix Mendelssohn's opera *Athaliah*, which asserts that the vicious woman acted in order "that no hand could reach out for her crown, nor king henceforth from David's line preserve again the service of Jehovah" (First Declamation).

Racine also ascribed to Athaliah a second motive, namely her sense of duty to protect the realm from the various enemies that surrounded it. Indeed, she boasts that her success in this effort was evidence of heaven's blessing on it (2.5.465–484). However, since it is unclear how the slaughter of her grandchildren contributed to the regional peace that Athaliah claimed as the fruit of her wisdom (2, 5), this explanation is not so plausible as the first.

The third motive ascribed by Racine seems more reasonable and is certainly more interesting—namely, that Athaliah acted out of vengeance for the recent killing of her mother and the rest of her own family. Deranged by wrath and loathing, she imagined that the slaughter of her posterity avenged the slaughter of her predecessors: "Yes, my just wrath, of which I am proud, has avenged my parents on my off-spring" (2.7.709–710).

This explanation, which I believe to be correct, makes no rational sense, however, except on the supposition that Athaliah blamed Israel's God for what befell her own family. In attacking David's house, she thought to attack David's God, whom she accuses of "implacable vengeance" (2.7.727).

In this respect, the third motive of Racine's Athaliah is the goal of the first. That is to say, the hateful queen seeks to destroy David's house in order to render void God's promises given through the prophets, especially the promise of the Messiah that would come from David's line, "that King promised to the nations, that Child of David, your hope, your expectation" (2, 7).

The queen's vengeance, which later appears in Handel's oratorio *Athalia*, correctly indicates the Christian meaning, the *sensus plenior*, of the Old Testament story. Waging war on great David's greater Son, Athaliah foreshadowed yet another usurper of the Davidic throne, hateful King Herod, who likewise ordered a large massacre of little boys in a vain effort to retain the crown that did not belong to him.

Afterword

NEAR THE BEGINNING of this book, I mentioned that it could be a much longer work than it is. Many bad examples from the Bible have been left out. I wrote nothing about Joab's murder of Abner, for instance, nor of Jezebel's treachery against Naboth. So much bloodshed and villainy has gone untold. Nothing has been said here of the vile deeds of Doeg, and no notice was taken of that incestuous adulteress who craved the head of John the Baptist.

Still, I think, it is time to stop this list. We began it with the mother of our race conversing, one day, with the Snake, and we finished with the story of Eve's distant daughter slaughtering her infant grandchildren asleep in their cribs. Gracious! Evil of this sort wears down the soul, and I suspect some readers, if they have come this far, may feel the spiritual fatigue mentioned by C. S. Lewis when he completed *The Screwtape Letters.*

Let us take stock, then, of what these stories have told us about the moral life. Chief among these, I submit, is the constant, lifelong need for spiritual vigilance.

This vigilance is required, first of all, because of the nature of the Enemy. How often should we remind ourselves that "our struggle (*pali*) is not against flesh and blood"? On the contrary, we share this universe with evil spirits endowed with intelligence much older than, and vastly superior to, our own—even "the rulers of the darkness of this age" (Eph. 6:10–12).

As long as we are in this life, it is a fact, not a fancy, that our souls are always under siege. "Be sober," wrote that chastened man who knew what he was talking about, "be vigilant, because your Adversary the Devil goes about like a roaring lion, seeking whom he may devour" (1 Pet. 5:8).

It was not all of a sudden, however, that "Satan put into the heart of Judas Iscariot" to betray the Savior of the world (John 13:2). Satan does not *suddenly* enter anyone's heart. He arrives there by degrees. A full year before the betrayal, around the time of the previous Passover (6:4), Jesus recognized that Satan was already at work on the soul of the betrayer. Observe carefully how that chapter closes: "'Did I not choose you, the twelve, and one of you is a devil?' He spoke of Judas Iscariot, Simon's son, for it was he who would betray him, being one of the twelve" (6:70).

It is instructive that this assessment of Judas comes at the end of the Bread of Life discourse, because the betrayal itself took place in the context of the Lord's Supper. In that account we read of the betrayer, "after the piece of bread, Satan entered him. Then Jesus said to him, 'What you do, do quickly'" (John 13:27).

Let us pay attention to the context. In our earliest and most constant forms of the Eucharistic rite, the Church takes explicit notice of Jesus' betrayal. The most ancient extant example comes from St. Paul, writing about twenty-five years after the event: "I received from the Lord that which I also delivered to you: that the Lord Jesus *on the night in which he was betrayed* took bread; and when he had given thanks, he broke it and said, 'Take, eat; this is my body'" (1 Cor. 11:23–24).

Paul's phrase, "the night in which he was betrayed," is recited in every single service of the Divine Liturgy according to either of our common rites. Orthodox Christians, as they celebrate the solemn anamnesis of that defining event, are warned about that ancient betrayal.

Nor does the Church permit them to forget—like Uzzah—the danger attached to such a high-voltage concentration of holiness: "Therefore whoever eats this bread or drinks the cup of the Lord in an unworthy manner will be guilty of the body and blood of the Lord" (1 Cor. 11:27). We have been duly warned.

In addition to the need for sustained vigilance, the bad examples from the Bible instruct us on the danger of playing to (and identifying ourselves by) our strengths, the peril attached to the passions, the prowling about of dark thoughts through the shadows of an undisciplined mind, a distrust of inherited moral norms, the disguised hazards inherent in popular movements, an unacknowledged disposition to arrogance and the pride of life, the enticements of political power, and the utter madness of friendship with the world.

About the Author

F ATHER PATRICK HENRY REARDON, now retired from active ministry, was the longtime priest of All Saints Orthodox Church in Chicago, Illinois, and serves as a senior editor of *Touchstone Magazine*. He is the author of *Christ in the Psalms* and *Christ in His Saints*, together with the books in the "Orthodox Christian Reflections" Bible commentary series.

We hope you have enjoyed and benefited from this book. Your financial support makes it possible to continue our nonprofit ministry both in print and online. Because the proceeds from our book sales only partially cover the costs of operating **Ancient Faith Publishing** and **Ancient Faith Radio**, we greatly appreciate the generosity of our readers and listeners. Donations are tax deductible and can be made at **www.ancientfaith.com.**

To view our other publications,
please visit our website:
store.ancientfaith.com

ANCIENT FAITH
RADIO

Bringing you Orthodox Christian music,
readings, prayers, teaching, and podcasts
24 hours a day since 2004 at
www.ancientfaith.com

www.ingramcontent.com/pod-product-compliance
Lightning Source LLC
Chambersburg PA
CBHW031419120626
46545CB00006B/2183

* 9 7 8 1 9 5 5 8 9 0 8 5 4 *